Akhenaten and the Religion of Light

Akhenaten
and the

Religion of Light

Erik Hornung

*translated from
the German by*
David Lorton

Cornell University Press
ITHACA AND LONDON

English translation first published 1999 by Cornell University Press
First printing, Cornell Paperbacks, 2001

Printed in the United States of America

Library of Congress Cataloging-in-Publication Data

Hornung, Erik.
    [Echnaton. English]
    Akhenaten and the religion of light / Erik Hornung ;
translated from the German by David Lorton.
       p. cm.
    Includes bibliographical references (p.   ) and index.
    ISBN 0-8014-3658-3 (cloth : alk. paper)
    ISBN 0-8014-8725-0 (pbk. : alk. paper)
    1. Egypt—Religion. 2. Sun worship—Egypt. 3. Akhenaten,
King of Egypt. I. Title.
    BL2443.H6613 1999
    299'.31—dc21   99-16166

Cornell University Press strives to use environmentally responsible
suppliers and materials to the fullest extent possible in the publishing of
its books. Such materials include vegetable-based, low-VOC inks and
acid-free papers that are recycled, totally chlorine-free, or partly
composed of nonwood fibers. Books that bear the logo of the FSC
(Forest Stewardship Council) use paper taken from forests that have been
inspected and certified as meeting the highest standards for
environmental and social responsibility. For further information, visit our
website at www.cornellpress.cornell.edu.

1 3 5 7 9   Cloth printing   10 8 6 4 2
3 5 7 9   Paperback printing   10 8 6 4 2

FOR ELISABETH STAEHELIN
JANUARY 3, 1995

Contents

Translator's Note

IN THIS EDITION, the following conventions have been adopted in the citations from ancient and modern texts:

Parentheses ( ) enclose words or brief explanations that have been added for clarity.

Square brackets [ ] enclose words that have been restored in a lacuna.

An ellipsis . . . indicates that a word or words in the original text have been omitted in the citation.

English-speaking Egyptologists have no single set of conventions for the rendering of ancient Egyptian and modern Arabic personal and place-names. Most of the names mentioned in this book occur in a standard reference work, John Baines and Jaromír Málek, *Atlas of Ancient Egypt* (New York: Facts on File, 1980), and the renderings here follow those in that volume. The only exception is the omission of the typographical sign for *ayin;* this consonant does not exist in English, and it was felt that its inclusion would serve only as a distraction to the reader.

In the texts at Amarna, Akhenaten's god is often called "the Aten," with the definite article, but sometimes also just "Aten." Both usages are reflected in the German edition of this book, and they are repeated here.

The citations from Thomas Mann in Chapter 1 are taken from *Joseph and His Brothers*, translated by Helen F. Lowe-Porter (New York: Knopf, 1948), pp. 971, 932.

In Chapter 6, the quotation from Johann Wolfgang von Goethe is taken from *Conversations with Eckermann: Being Appreciations and Criticisms on Many Subjects* (Washington, D.C.: M. Walter Dunne, 1901). For the citation from Carl Gustav Jung, see *Memories, Dreams, Reflections*, translated by Richard and Clara Winston (New York: Random House, 1963), p. 269.

Nearly all the Egyptian gods and goddesses mentioned in this book can be found in the "Glossary of Major Gods" in Dimitri Meeks and Christine Favard-Meeks, *Daily Life of the Egyptian Gods*, translated by G. M. Goshgarian (Ithaca: Cornell University Press, 1996), pp. 235–241. For the Egyptian monarchs and periods of Egyptian history, the reader is referred to the "Chronology" in Erik Hornung, *History of Ancient Egypt: An Introduction*, translated by David Lorton (Ithaca: Cornell University Press, 1999), pp. xiii–xix.

Akhenaten, his religion, and his times exert a never-ending fascination for scholars and laypeople alike. No other period attracts as much attention in the scholarly literature, and this fresh, up-to-date treatment is very much in order. I am grateful to Cornell University Press for having asked me to participate in this project, and I also wish to thank Prof. Hornung and Dr. Eckhard Eichler for their support and encouragement.

D. L.

Akhenaten and the Religion of Light

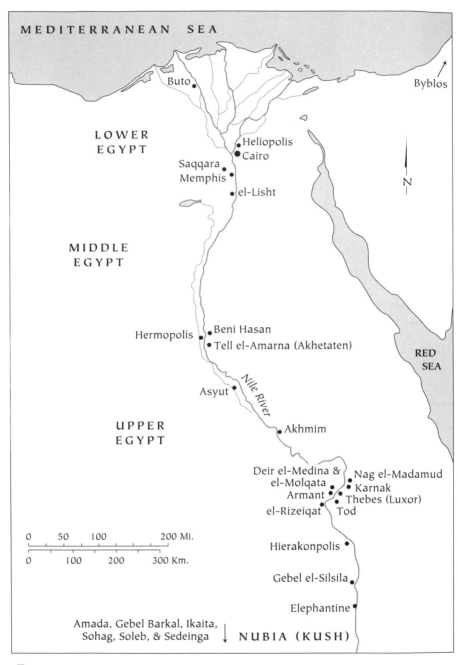

MEDITERRANEAN SEA

Byblos

Buto

LOWER
EGYPT

Heliopolis
Cairo
Saqqara
Memphis
el-Lisht

N

MIDDLE
EGYPT

Hermopolis
Beni Hasan
Tell el-Amarna (Akhetaten)

RED
SEA

Asyut

Nile River

UPPER
EGYPT

Akhmim

Deir el-Medina &
el-Molqata
Armant
el-Rizeiqat

Nag el-Madamud
Karnak
Thebes (Luxor)
Tod

Hierakonpolis

0   50   100   200 Mi.

0   100   200   300 Km.

Gebel el-Silsila

Elephantine

Amada, Gebel Barkal, Ikaita,
Sohag, Soleb, & Sedeinga   NUBIA (KUSH)

Egypt

1

The Founder of a Religion Is Discovered

Champollion's Impressions

During his first and only trip to Egypt, Jean-François Champollion at first planned on a very brief stay in Middle Egypt, the region between the two great ancient centers of Memphis and Thebes. He felt an urge to press forward as quickly as possible to the wondrous world of the temples and tombs of Upper Egypt. But the rock-cut tombs of Beni Hasan offered more than he had expected, and he spent two weeks there before continuing in great haste to Asyut, the largest city in Upper Egypt.

He had but a single day at the beginning of November 1828 for Tell el-Amarna, which was on the way and which he called "Psinaula." Here, as early as November 1714, the Jesuit father Claude Sicard had prepared rather fanciful copies of one of Akhenaten's boundary stelae, while the scholars of Bonaparte's expedition had discovered the remains of an ancient city at El-Till. Shortly before Champollion, in 1824, J. Gardner Wilkinson had discovered the tombs of Akhenaten's officials and made copies, but his accounts of his finds did not appear in print until several years after Champollion's death.

The latter had no time for the remote rock-cut tombs. He had only a brief look around the city itself and made some disconcerted notes in front of the boundary stelae: "King very fat and swollen, big belly. Feminine contours . . . *grande morbidezza* [considerable softness]." In the summary of Egyptian history which was included as an appendix to the publication of his letters from Egypt, Champollion proceeded immediately from Amenophis III to his son "Horus," who continued the work of his father but had two weak successors, after which Sethos I led Egypt to new and brilliant heights.

Thus the founder of Egyptology had no knowledge of Akhenaten and his far-reaching revolution aside from some fleeting impressions regarding the distinctive quality of the art of his period as contrasted to the traditional style. But even this insight already marked a step forward, because there were no examples of Amarna art in European collections prior to 1826.

It was only around the middle of the nineteenth century that Wilkinson and Lepsius laid the foundations of our knowledge of the Amarna Period, when ancient Egyptian culture and religion were fundamentally transformed for several years, and which even witnessed the introduction of a new literary language, and during which a religion was *founded* for the first time in the history of the world. To the best of our knowledge, this had never happened before, either in Egypt or elsewhere.

Lepsius Discovers the Founder

Karl Richard Lepsius arrived at Tell el-Amarna on September 19, 1843, with the expedition sent by the Prussian king, Friedrich Wilhelm IV. He spent three days there, and another seven in June 1845 on his journey back from Upper Egypt and

Nubia. Like Wilkinson before him, he worked primarily in
the tombs, making numerous drawings, squeezes, and plaster
casts. He communicated the first results of his research to
the learned world in his letters from Egypt; thus, in a letter
written to Alexander von Humboldt on November 20, 1843,
he correctly observed that "Bech-en-Aten" was not a
woman, as he had at first thought. Nestor l'Hôte, who visited Amarna a few years earlier, had also been uncertain
whether Akhenaten was a man or a woman. The feminine
appearance of his representations, as already noted by Champollion, together with a tradition preserved by Manetho, a
historian of the Ptolemaic Period, had led to this misappre-
hension. Akhenaten again made his appearance as a woman
in book 3 of the influential work by Christian C. J. Bunsen,
Aegyptens Stelle in der Weltgeschichte [Egypt's place in universal history] (Hamburg, 1845), pp. 88–90. "Amentuanch,"
known to us today as Tutankhamun, also appeared there,
though as a sort of Nubian counterking of the period and
with his historical role thus thoroughly misrepresented. In
book 4, which appeared in 1856, "Aachenaten" was correctly
identified as a man (pp. 162–164).

Some years after his return from Egypt, on June 26, 1851,
Lepsius communicated his conclusions at a meeting of the
Prussian Academy of Sciences in Berlin, and later that year
he also made them known in print, in a monograph titled
*Ueber den ersten ägyptischen Götterkreis und seine geschichtlich-
mythologische Entstehung* [On the earliest Egyptian pantheon
and its historical and mythological origin]. In this treatise, he
spoke of a "highly noteworthy episode in the history of
Egyptian mythology," in which Amenophis IV (whose identity with Akhenaten was now secure) opposed the prior worship of Amun with a "pure cult of the sun": "only the disk
itself was tolerated as its unique image." Additionally, he

commanded that "the names of all the deities be hacked away from all public monuments, and even from the accessible private tombs, and that their images be destroyed to the extent possible" (p. 197; p. 41 of the reprint edition). After a few years, however, there followed a "reaction on the part of the old national hierarchy," which obliterated the memory of the religious zealot. Finally, Lepsius expressed uncertainty regarding "what special circumstances might have emboldened a legitimate pharaoh to attempt such a total change in the deeply rooted religious tradition of a great and advanced people" (p. 202; p. 46). Possibilities he considered were that influences from Nubia or western Asia lay in the background, and that worship of the sun belonged to the most ancient roots of the "polymorphic polytheism of Egypt."

Vague Recollections in Antiquity

Lepsius was not fully conscious of the consequences of his discovery; it is only in retrospect that he is, for us, the one who recovered Akhenaten and his religion for modern times. He had happened upon the founder of a religion, one entirely forgotten for millennia! The work of Manetho, who in the third century B.C.E. wrote a history of Egypt that was considered authoritative from antiquity down to modern times, displays no clear knowledge of Akhenaten's reign. For Manetho, the Ramessides were the immediate successors of Amenophis III. Herodotus, Diodorus, Strabo, and the other classical writers also had no knowledge of Akhenaten and his times. But Manetho handed down a story, preserved by Josephus, according to which lepers, led by the priest Osarsiph, ruled over Egypt in league with the Hyksos for thirteen years during the reign of "Amenophis" (Amenophis III). Taking all the sacred animals with him, King Amenophis went to

Ethiopia, whence he freed Egypt after thirteen years and expelled the lepers. Meanwhile, the lepers had burned the cities, destroyed the temples and the statues of the gods, and even roasted the sacred animals on spits. In all this, there is doubtless influence from later experiences of foreign rule on the part of the Egyptians, especially the Assyrian and Persian conquests of their land. But Manetho also had knowledge of an early religious conflict, and in comparing it with sickness (leprosy; in Diodorus, a plague), he adopts a metaphor already employed by Tutankhamun on his "Restoration Stela" in describing the period before he came to the throne: "The land experienced an illness, and the deities did not look after this land." But neither of them mentions the "heretic king" by name; he had already been suppressed by his immediate successors, after which he was forgotten.

How did this total oblivion come about? Akhenaten's revolution was not put down by force. Egyptians went on to do other things, and they simply forgot it, though it continued to have effects in undercurrents. It was once thought that King Haremhab was the "liquidator" of the Amarna Period, but it seems that Sethos I and Ramesses II were the first to turn actively against Akhenaten and his immediate successors; they were deleted from the king lists, and the divine names that had been hacked out were restored, as were the representations of Amun. The disruptions unleashed by the reformer were now overcome, and responses were found to his provocations; his reign could thus be thoroughly forgotten. The notion of remnants of a "community" of devotees of the Aten has proved to be an attractive literary motif, but it is highly unlikely that there was such a thing in the historical situation around 1300 B.C.E. The new religion had no martyrs: there was no reason to persecute it, for it had survived Akhenaten by only a few years. What followed was total oblivion, after a brief, vague recollection of the "sinner of Akhetaten." It is symbolic that the tomb of Tutankhamun was buried under the rubble from the later tomb of Ramesses VI, with the result that it was preserved, along with its treasure.

Bringing this period and the religious founder back to life, rescuing them from oblivion, has thus been an accomplishment of modern scholarship, one whose influence continues to resonate. Today, the Amarna Period is regarded as the most exciting epoch in Egyptian history, and it serves as the framework and background for most modern novels and stories set in ancient Egypt. Akhenaten himself cannot be omitted from any intellectual history of humankind, and he and his accomplishments are continually reassessed. The sixteen years of his reign demonstrate impressively how the tempo of historical development more than three thousand years ago could approximate that of modern times.

The Discovery Is Completed

But let us return to the reaction to Akhenaten in the nineteenth century! From the title of the treatise published by the Prussian Academy of Sciences, in which Lepsius published his insights into the reign of Akhenaten in 1851, one would hardly suspect what new and pioneering historical insights it contained. But academic treatises were read by the entire educated world at that time, with the result that neither Egyptologists nor general historians could ignore Lepsius's discoveries, though several years would pass before the first reaction to them. Thanks to the collaboration of Thomas Schneider, it is possible to offer some indications here regarding their earliest reception.

In the second, corrected and expanded edition of his much read *Geschichte des Alterthums* [History of antiquity], vol. 1

(Berlin, 1855), Maximilian Duncker still knew nothing of Akhenaten; it was only in the third edition of 1863 that he treated the Amarna Period, following the account by Heinrich Brugsch, to which we shall turn shortly. The first writer of a history of the world who knew of Akhenaten and his significance was thus Georg Weber, in his *Allgemeinen Weltgeschichte mit besonderer Berücksichtigung des Geistes- und Culturlebens der Völker und mit Benutzung der neueren geschichtlichen Forschungen für die gebildeten Stände* [General world history . . .], whose first volume, *Geschichte des Morgenlandes* [History of the East], appeared in Leipzig in 1857, six years after Lepsius's contribution.

Aside from Lepsius, Duncker and the general historians who succeeded him were able to make use of the first history of pharaonic Egypt that was consistently based on contemporary sources and not solely on classical authors. This history was first published by Heinrich Brugsch in French in 1859; he treated the "Period of Religious Reformation" in a section of its own (pp. 118–123) and provided a summary of Lepsius's work and insights. Meanwhile Lepsius had reproduced the reliefs from the rock tombs of Amarna in his great *Denkmäler aus Aegypten und Nubien* [Monuments of Egypt and Nubia], thus considerably expanding the available material. Brugsch dealt with the religious reforms and the "single god" of Akhenaten, drawing the still popular parallel between Aten and Adonis and mentioning the "hymns filled with poetic ideas" and the unusual manner in which the king was depicted, which had already struck Champollion. He followed Lepsius in assuming that Akhenaten had been a priest of Re before coming to the throne, and he thought it important that the reformer's mother, Teye, was not a member of the royal house—her "bourgeois" parents, Yuya and Tuya, were known from the famous "marriage scarab" of Amenophis III long before the discovery of their tomb in the Valley of the Kings in 1905. Akhenaten's successor seemed to be Aya; Tutankhamun, who for a long time was known only from the Theban tomb of Huy, his Viceroy of Kush, appeared to be the latter's successor.

The correct order of Akhenaten's successors—Tutankhamun and then Aya—was established in the German edition of the work, which first appeared in Leipzig in 1877 under the title *Geschichte Aegypten's unter den Pharaonen, nach den Denkmaelern* [A history of Egypt under the pharaohs derived entirely from the monuments]. There, Brugsch again stressed (pp. 419–421) that Akhenaten had been handicapped by the "bad marriage" of his father to a "foreigner," and that his "documented aversion . . . to the worship of Amun, the revered national god, and his divine circle, was to be blamed on the daughter of foreigners," his mother Teye, who had planted the "teaching of a *single* god of light [in him] when he was a tender youth." The "heresy" and the "unseemly" appearance of the king served to strengthen the revulsion against him. Driven from Thebes by the displeasure of the priests and the people, he was obliged to seek a new capital; his marital bliss was his compensation for the rejection he had met at their hands.

The "Heretic" as Precursor of Modern Ideas

At the end of this overwhelmingly negative depiction, Brugsch found some quite positive things to say, thus differing from Lepsius. He spoke (p. 427) of the "depth of (Akhenaten's) thought" and the "inner devotion" that appear in the inscriptions in the tombs of Tell el-Amarna, such "that one is almost inclined to applaud the teaching of which the king speaks so often and eagerly." Brugsch was thus already on the way to viewing Akhenaten as a "modern" and "enlightened" monarch.

In the same year, there appeared the German edition of Gaston Maspero's *Histoire des peuples de l'Orient* [History of the peoples of the Orient], which in its several editions had been the authoritative account of pharaonic history in the French language. Maspero followed some of Mariette's ideas, among them that Akhenaten had been castrated during his father's Nubian campaign. In later editions, he held the view that the negative opinion of modern historians had served to fulfill the Theban priests' curse on Akhenaten, with the result that a negative recollection of him had replaced the former oblivion. For Maspero, Teye was no longer a foreigner, and he was the first to take Akhenaten's Great Hymn to the Aten into consideration, though he did not offer a complete translation.

After the detailed accounts by Lepsius, Brugsch, and Maspero, Akhenaten was no longer unknown to historians or educated people generally; but to Weber and Duncker, he remained a marginal figure, a reformer of the existing order whose work did not survive him and who inaugurated a period of decline after the brilliant reigns of his predecessors. As late as 1881, Leopold von Ranke made no mention of him in his *Weltgeschichte* [World history], whereas he was quite familiar with the ephemeral Tutankhamun because of the "Negro queen" and the tribute scenes in the tomb of the Viceroy Huy. Eduard Meyer thus felt obliged to reproach Ranke for having "almost entirely ignored the results of the scholarly work of half a century."

Eduard Meyer's *Geschichte des Altertums* [History of the ancient world], which first appeared in Stuttgart in 1884, offered the most detailed account of pharaonic history that had ever been written, and in its successive editions it was continually improved, taking into account the most recent research, including that on the Amarna Period. But it was not until 1910 that a monograph entirely devoted to the "heretic king" appeared: Arthur Weigall's *The Life and Times of Akhnaton, Pharaoh of Egypt* (Edinburgh, 1910; 2d ed., London, 1922).

New Archaeological Finds

Before we turn to Weigall and his portrayal of Akhenaten, let us review some milestones in the history of the archaeological work done at Amarna subsequent to Lepsius's expedition. The king's tomb at Tell el-Amarna was found by local Egyptians in 1881–82, though it was not investigated by the Antiquities Service until the 1890s; some of the objects from the burial equipment were found only in 1931–32, when a fresh clearance of the tomb was made. In 1887 it was once again locals who discovered the famed archive of clay tablets containing the cuneiform correspondence of Akhenaten and his father with the princes of western Asia. About 380 tablets are preserved, and their contents were translated in the still authoritative edition by J. A. Knudtzon in 1915. This sensational find led to the first systematic excavations at Akhenaten's capital; these were carried out by W. M. Flinders Petrie in 1891–92 with the assistance of the young Howard Carter, and the results were published soon afterward.

The famed Great Hymn to the Aten was studied for the first time in 1895 by the American James Henry Breasted in his Berlin University dissertation, *De Hymnis in Solem sub Rege Amenophide IV conceptis* [On the hymns to the sun composed under King Amenophis IV]; luckily, Bouriant had already made a copy of it in 1883–84 before about a third of the text, which is in the tomb of Aya, was maliciously destroyed in 1890. Thanks to translations by Breasted,

Griffith, Maspero, and Erman, this text—which has often been compared to the "Canticle of the Sun" of St. Francis of Assisi, and even to Psalm 104—was widely known at the outset of the twentieth century and has ever since been considered an integral part of world literature. Additionally, it remains perhaps the most important source for the religion of Akhenaten.

In 1901 Norman de Garis Davies began his work in the tombs at Amarna, which he published in six volumes from 1903 to 1908; to this day, his *Rock Tombs of El Amarna* remains one of the most important bases for any investigation of this period. In 1907, in the course of his excavations in the Valley of the Kings, Theodore Davis discovered tomb 55, which contained a mummy that was long held to be that of Akhenaten. The conviction that the mortal remains of the religious reformer were finally in hand prompted Weigall to write his book, which he expressly dedicated to the "Discoverer of the bones of Akhenaton."

The excavations of the German Oriental Society at Tell el-Amarna began in 1911, under the direction of Ludwig Borchardt. They were brought to an end by World War I, but not before rich finds were made, especially (in 1912) the bust of Nefertiti in a sculptor's workshop. The division of the finds, which was later disputed, occurred on January 20, 1913; the bust went to Berlin, though it was not exhibited until after the war. The Egypt Exploration Society continued the excavations at the site from 1921 to 1936, with considerable— though less spectacular—results. These English excavations were resumed much later, in 1977.

The discovery of the tomb of Tutankhamun by Howard Carter in 1922 had a lasting impact. Everyone was now talking about the Amarna Period, and there was a tremendous response to the discovery in the media of the day, but it also stimulated works of literature about this newly revealed period. The most important was *Joseph and His Brothers* by Thomas Mann, but there were others, among them a free rendering of the Great Hymn to the Aten by Franz Werfel. There was a further discovery in 1925–26, that of the unusual colossi of Akhenaten at Karnak, which are important evidence for the beginnings of his "expressionistic" art.

With that, the series of spectacular discoveries came to an end, though our sources have steadi'y increased in the meanwhile. Since the 1920s, tens of thousands of decorated blocks have been recovered from many of the structures at Karnak, and from other nearby sanctuaries as well, and these have shed light on the beginnings of Akhenaten's religious and artistic revolution. From a later period of the reign come the sources regarding the king's Nubian campaign, which call his alleged pacifism into question, as well as evidence of his favorite, Kiya, a rival of Nefertiti and her daughters. Another surprising discovery was that of a new vizier of Asiatic origin, Aper-El, whose tomb at Saqqara was found by Alain Zivie in 1980.

A New Religion Comes to Light

In his *History of Egypt,* which appeared in many editions from 1894 on, W. M. Flinders Petrie, the excavator of Amarna, had very positive words for the king's religion, which stands up to even the most modern requirements: "If this were a new religion, invented to satisfy our modern scientific conceptions, we could not find a flaw in the correctness of this view of the energy of the solar system . . . a position which we cannot logically improve upon at the present day" (p. 214).

Adolf Erman expressed himself more critically in his account of Egyptian religion, which appeared in 1905. He stressed the "strangely sick appearance of the king" and his "fanaticism"; for him, Akhenaten was an "enlightened despot," and he concluded by remarking, "But as pretty as it is thought to be, his new art bears as unhealthy a streak as his new religion, and neither was capable of surviving" (p. 71). In the third edition of 1934, Erman devoted an entire chapter to the "heretical period," expressing himself there somewhat more positively.

Breasted, on the other hand, saw in Akhenaten a "'God-intoxicated man,' whose mind responded with marvellous sensitiveness and discernment to the visible evidences of God about him. He was fairly ecstatic in his sense of the beauty of the eternal and universal light." He noted the modernity of Akhenaten's teaching and its anticipation of Christian attitudes and beliefs, but he also stressed the king's inadequate comprehension of the practical needs of his realm and his "fanaticism."

The First Biography and Its Influence

Arthur Weigall, the first biographer of this religious innovator, followed Breasted in his opinion that Akhenaten was "the world's first idealist and the world's first individual"; he was, moreover, the first to found a religion, and he established a "religion so pure that we must compare it to Christianity in order to discover its faults" (p. 62). Weigall otherwise stresses that no other religion so closely resembles Christianity (p. 147), and he compares the icon of the sun disk with its rays to the Christian cross and the Great Hymn to the Aten to Psalm 104 and St. Francis of Assisi (pp. 155–157).

In this book, which Kurt Sethe classified as "novelistic," Weigall laid the foundation for an idyllic view of the Aten religion, Akhenaten's family life, and life in general in his new

Residence, all this in stark contrast to the terrible events in western Asia which could be reconstructed from Akhenaten's cuneiform archive. Akhenaten as a pacifist who ruined Egypt as a world power in Dynasty 18, as a king caught up in the unreal, sham world of the Horizon of Aten, his new capital, where he lived out his teaching and conducted his search for the divine—these were clichés that would have long-lasting influence. Though Thomas Mann overcame these clichés in his nuanced treatment of the king, he succumbed to the parallels with Christianity and attempted to categorize Akhenaten as an early Christ figure.

At the end of his portrayal, Weigall presents a rather dramatic characterization of Akhenaten's utter failure. In every area, the king's domestic and foreign policies foundered: his teaching came to naught, his empire collapsed, and loyal vassals like Ribaddi of Byblos (even he was to become a cliché!) experienced defeat notwithstanding their constant appeals for help. Akhenaten became a tragic figure, an unappreciated and failed precursor of Christ—"right on the way, and yet not the right one for the way," as Thomas Mann put it in his well-known formula.

No biography that has appeared in the meanwhile has exercised as much influence as Weigall's book did on his contemporaries and on the generations that followed. Though we are obliged to regard Lepsius as the scholar who discovered Akhenaten after millennia of oblivion, we must acknowledge Weigall as the one who established him definitively in the consciousness of the modern era and identified him as a great teacher in human history. In 1952 Rudolf Anthes paraphrased the attitude that originated with Breasted and Weigall:

> Thirty years ago, perhaps all of us saw (Amarna religion) under the influence of J. H. Breasted. It was the highest and the purest flowering of insight into the divine in Egypt. Akhenaten had freed

himself from the mumbo-jumbo of the traditional religion. He had found a direct path from the human to the divine. He rejected myths, symbols, and everything polytheistic. Since he was not accorded a revelation of God, he saw Him in the sun; but light, life, and truth guided him . . . (and) on an unprecedented level of insight, he anticipated basic concepts of the Gospel according to St. John. To us, Akhenaten seemed to have been the prophet of a religion for which his time was not yet ripe.

A little later in his monograph, Anthes again notes Akhenaten's "rationalism," which speaks directly to "our times."

Today, it is his monotheism which we especially value as evidence of progress and an anticipation of the great universal religions. In his late work *Moses and Monotheism,* Sigmund Freud characterized Moses as an Egyptian who transmitted Akhenaten's religion to the tribes of Israel, and even in Islam there are voices that lay claim to Akhenaten as a precursor. For others, his "enlightened" reform is not to be viewed as the establishment of a religion but rather as a philosophy of nature, an anticipation of Thales or even of Einstein.

Critical Notes Are Sounded

Since World War II, there have been scholars who have viewed Akhenaten less positively and as less of a revolutionary. Like Rudolf Anthes, Kurt Lange (1951) remained fully positive, but for Eberhard Otto (1953), the king was "a particularly unpolitical and egocentric man, ugly and sickly, ambitious and despotic. Nature had not endowed him with the means of realizing his need for esteem with warlike deeds, like Tuthmosis III, or physical prowess, like Amenophis II, or pasha-like hedonism, like Amenophis III; but since, like his predecessors, he strove for fulfillment, the king's need drove him with the same intensity and extremism to the fulfillment of an idea." According to Otto, the king adhered to the status quo; only his intolerance was novel. Moreover, for Otto, Akhenaten's "making a public spectacle of the private life of royalty . . . seen from the ancient Egyptian point of view, was absolutely tasteless and aberrant"; Breasted had given these "charmingly natural and unrestrained relations with his family" a thoroughly positive evaluation.

Joachim Spiegel (1950) attempted to characterize Akhenaten as an imitator who emulated the far more important revolution at the end of the Old Kingdom; for Spiegel, he represented the "Egyptian form of enlightenment," subscribing to a cult of reason, though he was also shaped by the "pathological grotesqueness of his physical form." Fixated on his notion of "axial periods," Karl Jaspers (1949) was entirely blind to the importance of Akhenaten's religion, for in his view early cultures "were lacking in spiritual revolutions" and were "not much spiritually moved." He makes no explicit mention of Akhenaten, who proves such assertions to be unfounded, but he doubtless has him in mind when he says elsewhere, "In fleeting signs, we see astonishing anticipations, as though a breakthrough was about to begin but never occurred, especially in Egypt."

Eric Voegelin, on the other hand, treated the reformer at length in the first volume of his great work, *Order and History* (Baton Rouge, 1956, pp. 101–110), noting "the modern atmosphere of individualism" and rating Akhenaten as the first religious reformer "clearly distinguishable as an individual" in the history of humankind. In the fourth volume (1974, p. 283), he returned to the "extraordinary personality of Akhenaton," stressing his cosmopolitan outlook. For Gerardus van der Leeuw, who published a book on Akhenaten in Dutch in 1927, the king was even "one of the greatest people in the history of the world."

Evaluations of Akhenaten continue to fluctuate between

the two extremes among the most recent writers, and they are rather negative in the biographies by Cyril Aldred and Donald B. Redford—the latter judges him to be "no intellectual heavyweight." Siegfried Morenz sees "terror from above and careerism from below" in the reign of Akhenaten, and according to Jan Assmann, his actions were characterized by "unheard-of brutality." The title "Hero or Heretic" given to a symposium on Akhenaten in New York City at the beginning of December 1990 attempted to capture the extent to which opinions have differed.

Not in the Mists of Later Legends

In any event, one thing fundamentally distinguishes Akhenaten from the founders of other religions. While we can be certain that our knowledge of Buddha, Jesus, and Mohammed will never be enriched by fresh contemporary sources, nearly every year brings new sources and fresh insights into Akhenaten, new details regarding his character and his influence. He is a religious founder who visibly grows and changes, continually displaying new traits; but along with him, his teaching also grows, and, as it gains in clarity, it seems to belong to the future perhaps rather more than to the past. And in contrast to the founders of all other religions, Akhenaten is not shrouded in the mists of later legends; all that we have of him is contemporary and goes back to the man himself. His teaching is revealed to us by him alone, with no intermediaries, and it is subject to falsification only by modern interpretations.

Before we turn to this teaching and attempt to expound it, we must ask: Who was Akhenaten, and what do we know of his personality? In defiance of all hopes, we do not have his mummy, and we cannot draw conclusions regarding his appearance from representations of him in the art. As we have seen, Lepsius at first took him for a woman, a view still held by Eugène Lefébure long after Lepsius's death. To Mariette and Maspero, he was a eunuch, while for Weigall and a number of others, he was an epileptic; Elliot Smith concluded that he was hydrocephalic, while Pillet saw an artificial deformation of the back of his head; Moret suggested "premature old age," and Aldred proposed Fröhlich's Syndrome. Several physicians have attempted a more precise determination of his symptoms.

In his book on Akhenaten, Aldred devotes an entire chapter to this "medical" explanation of the king. Taken together with his extreme assumption of a lengthy coregency with his father, which many scholars hold to this day, a totally absurd picture results: a physically and psychologically unsound person was allowed to bring his eccentric ideas to fruition for twelve years while he shared the throne with his father, who was seriously ill, only to have the instruments of power taken away from him again, like a child! More plausible is Thomas Mann's description of his appearance as that of "an aristocratic young Englishman of somewhat decadent stock"— "pretty and well-favored . . . not at all, but of a disturbing attractiveness."

The fact that we have a large number of contemporary representations of this first known founder of a religion helps us only indirectly in forming a picture of his appearance and his character traits. And since Egyptian royal portraits tended to depict monarchs in the prime of youth, we can only conclude from the length of his father's reign that he could not have been much younger than twenty at the beginning of his own rule. If we wish to know him personally, we can only consider his teaching and the roots from which it sprang.

2

The Religious Background

The New Solar Theology

The religious ideas with which Akhenaten grew up were those of the "New Solar Theology," which Jan Assmann in particular has investigated. It is to be encountered in hymns and rituals and in the Books of the Netherworld of Dynasty 18. At its core is the daily course of the sun, which guarantees the continued existence of the cosmos. The sun god renews his creation every morning, but he also descends nightly into the netherworld, where his revivifying light wakes the dead to new life in the depths of the earth. The entire cosmos is dependent upon light and the sight of the god, but this light must be continually regenerated in the darkness; it must overcome dangers and hostile forces whose most powerful embodiment is the enormous serpent Apopis.

These menacing forces are defeated, and the New Solar Theology reflects a deep trust in the reliability of the sun. This god, whose visible cult image was the sun and whom the Egyptians worshiped under several names, was the creator of the other gods; he was thus the unique god of the gods, hidden and inscrutable in his essence, and therefore especially worshiped as Amun, whose name means "Hidden One." The remoteness of the god is constantly stressed, though he was also immanent in his rays. The visible light on which all creation depended shone upon a world filled with mythic concepts, which Akhenaten would eliminate in their entirety.

The creator renewed his work each night in the depths of the netherworld, where he effected his own regeneration and at the same time wakened the dead to new life. Setting each evening, he had a share in the fate of death; in the course of the New Kingdom, it became customary to view Osiris, god of the dead, as a form of the sun god, so that he ruled not only this world but the next one as well. Next to this omnipotent luminary, the other divine powers ran the risk of fading into insignificance.

His Father's Policies

It appears that Amenophis III tried to prevent this single god from gaining the upper hand by stressing the multiplicity of deities in Egypt, especially in connection with his festival of renewal. In addition to the series of Sakhmet statues he commissioned a further series of statues, on whose bases he was designated as "beloved" of a very great variety of deities, among them less important and specifically local ones. Similar epithets occur on an extensive series of large scarabs connecting the king with numerous deities. There were definitely tendencies—and not only at the royal court—that ran counter to the New Solar Theology and its elevation of a single god over the entire pantheon in a manner that was altogether too one-sided and, in that respect, un-Egyptian.

But the plurality of deities was not replaced in principle

by this unique and distant sun god, and they remained in existence along with the Aten in the early years of Akhenaten. From a modern, strictly logical point of view, it would take only one small step to turn this unique god, this god of all gods, into a single one who tolerated no other deity besides himself. Akhenaten in fact took this step, though only as the final consequence of his reflections concerning the divine and the gods. First, however, he made a *religion* (as Jan Assmann observes) out of the New Solar Theology with which he had grown up, and this will be the topic of Chapter 4.

Politically, the reign of Amenophis III was a period of stability and peace; Akhenaten's grandfather, Tuthmosis IV, had laid the foundations for it by bringing an end to the decades of military conflict between the two great powers of that era. The other power was the kingdom of Mitanni, whose center lay in the border area between Syria and Iraq, and whose struggles with Egypt concerned control over northern Syria, which was a matter of exercising sovereignty over the princes there. During the reign of Akhenaten, the Hittite kingdom in Anatolia would establish itself as yet another great power and intervene in this area.

Amenophis III had led only two rather symbolic campaigns into Nubia, while he maintained Egypt's power in western Asia solely through diplomacy, marriage alliances, and rich consignments of gold and other products. Egypt perceived itself as a world power, and Pharaoh's court became an international center where ambassadors of all lands came and went, where goods from Asia and Crete were prized, and where even Asiatic deities such as Reshef, Baal, Astarte, and Qudshu were worshiped. The geographical horizons of the Egyptians now also encompassed the more important cities of the Aegean, as shown by a list of place-names from the king's mortuary temple. The prevailing atmosphere was one of openness to the outside world and receptiveness toward other religions. A scene in the fifth hour of the night in the Book of Gates, which originated at this time, places even the "wretched" Asiatics, Nubians, and Libyans under the protection of Egyptian deities in the afterlife, just as the Great Hymn to the Aten would stress the care of Akhenaten's god for foreign peoples.

Amenophis III was one of the greatest builders in the history of Egypt. Witness to this is borne especially by the temple of Luxor, by the double temple of Soleb and Sedeinga in Nubia, and by his mortuary temple on the west bank of Thebes; the latter exceeded all its predecessors in size, but it was soon severely damaged by an earthquake. Where the monumental entrance to the temple once stood, now only the two huge Colossi of Memnon, each more than sixty-five feet in height and weighing 720 tons (Figure 1), testify to the temple's original size, as well as to the king's tendency to megalomania. The latter stamped not only his architecture and royal statuary but other objects as well; never had such large *shawabti*s or scarabs been made. The officials of the royal court followed the king in this tendency, as shown above all by the huge, though uncompleted, tomb of the vizier Amenhotpe on the Asasif.

The tendency to the colossal was complemented by a turn to unusual building materials. In a dedicatory inscription at the temple of Montu in the Karnak complex, the king mentions precious materials such as gold, silver, lapis lazuli, jasper, turquoise, bronze, and copper, which he used in its construction and decoration, noting with pride the exact weights of each. He attempted thus to capture quite literally the "weight of this monument," as the caption to another list on the Third Pylon at Karnak puts it.

FIGURE I. *The Colossi of Memnon during the Nile inundation (1959)
and during the dry season. Photos by E. Hornung.*

The Royal Sed-Festival

There seems to have been a *sed*-festival for as long as there was a pharaoh. Representations of the king running the festival's course or sitting enthroned in its chapel occur on sealings from the beginning of the pharaonic period, c. 3000 B.C.E. These were two of the festival's most important rites, and they would be depicted again and again in later times.

The object of the festival was a renewal of the reigning monarch, whose power had become depleted over time, thus endangering the continued existence of the state. Instead of killing him and replacing him with a new ruler, it was considered sufficient to effect a symbolic burial of the "old" king in the form of a statue and accord him the opportunity to repeat his coronation and continue to reign as a "new" king. The ritual course he ran before all the deities of the land also symbolized the continued strength that qualified him for the renewal of his rulership.

In the Middle and New Kingdoms, this festival of renewal was celebrated before the end of the thirtieth year of rule and then repeated at briefer intervals of three or four years; in the case of Ramesses II, with his extremely long reign of over sixty-six years, we know of a dozen repetitions. In Egypt, thirty years was a round number signifying a generation, though our sources do not as yet permit a confirmation of this criterion for the Old Kingdom and the Late Period.

Amenophis III, though, affords us the most abundant attestation of an actual *sed*-festival in the thirtieth regnal year, for many dated inscriptions are preserved on vessels from his palace at el-Malqata, on the west bank of Thebes; these were part of the deliveries of supplies for the king's *sed*-festival and its repetitions. Akhenaten, who ruled less than thirty years and evidently celebrated his festival shortly after the beginning of his reign, is one of the few exceptions to the usual rule; this unusual celebration might have been connected with the theocracy of the Aten. In any case, this does not seem to have been a fictitious festival.

In many other cases, mention of a *sed*-festival does not constitute evidence for an actual celebration. Every pharaoh hoped to complete thirty years of rule and to be regenerated in a *sed*-festival, often articulating this wish in formulaic expressions from the very beginning of his reign; real celebrations of the festival cannot be inferred from such statements. Kings especially counted on continuing their festivals of renewal after their deaths—thus, for example, the young Tutankhamun was wished "millions of years and hundreds of thousands of *sed*-festivals"—and inscriptions containing such wishes were often carved on buildings dedicated to their continued existence.

Pharaoh wore a special vestment during most of the ceremonies of the festival, a mantle-like garment that also distinguished statues prepared for the *sed*-festival from other statues. Akhenaten affords the earliest example of a god who was also able to celebrate a *sed*-festival; later, Osiris in particular was included in its symbolism, for the desired regeneration played a special role in his case. Otherwise, however, the festival was a renewal of rulership, a purely royal festival; officials participated as supernumeraries, but they could celebrate no *sed*-festivals of their own.

On the criteria for the celebration of a sed-*festival, see E. Hornung and E. Staehelin,* Studien zum Sedfest, Aegyptiaca Helvetica 1 *(Geneva, 1974).*

The Festival of the Elder King

In spite of everything, Amenophis III was not an "enlightened" and irreligious monarch; rather, he was deeply rooted in traditional piety. His last decade was characterized by multiple celebrations of the great royal festival of renewal, the *sed*-festival, which was supposed to revive and ritually renew the waning powers of a king after thirty years of rule; it was then repeated at briefer intervals of three years each. Since he ruled a full thirty-eight years, Amenophis III was able to celebrate two repetitions before his death. All three celebrations took place in his palace at el-Malqata on the west bank of Thebes, and they are richly attested through deliveries that arrived there in inscribed and often dated jars. Japanese excavations have even uncovered a podium for a throne, whose thirty steps stand for the thirty years that had gone by; representations from all periods show that at the midpoint of the festival, Pharaoh sat enthroned on such a podium, thus repeating his coronation.

While a specific deification of the king was connected with the festival, every pharaoh was already divine. In the New Kingdom, this divinity was viewed above all as solar: the king not only was the "son of Re" but was himself the sun, lighting the world and playing the role of the sun god on earth through his deeds. Quite like Ramesses II at a later date, Amenophis III went a step further and had statues erected in which he was revered as a god—specifically, the sun god—during his lifetime; thus, there exist cult scenes in which the king is portrayed praying or making offerings to his own image! Thanks to a find of statues in the temple of Luxor a few years ago, we now have a statue that is actually an image of an image, depicting the cult statue of the deified king on a transport sledge.

Amenophis fell back on ancient models for the celebration

of his festival, but he took special care to raise it to new splendor. The ritual rejuvenation of rulership it was supposed to effect is documented by statues from the end of his reign which depict him with pronouncedly youthful features. He called himself the Dazzling Sun, while at his side his chief wife, Teye, played the role of Hathor, the companion of the sun god who stood for all aspects of regeneration. The bourgeois origin of Queen Teye was constantly stressed, and she was called a "simple girl," though her parents, Yuya and Tuya, evidently belonged to an influential and important family from the region of Akhmim, with which the royal house had allied itself several times. Teye played an unusually prominent role in both politics and religion. Amuletic seals bearing her name were widespread, and she even enjoyed the confidence of Asiatic kings, while in Nubia she shared in the divine worship received by her husband.

The marriages of Amenophis III to his daughters—the ones in question are Sitamun and (doubtfully) Isis—are most likely connected with his first *sed*-festival: a "new" king probably also needed a "new" chief wife, though the rights and status of Teye were in no way diminished. The important role played by the royal family in the late years of Amenophis III calls to mind the prominence it would have in the Amarna Period, though the relaxed intimacy of the scenes from the latter period are missing from the art of Amenophis. It is striking, though, that the later "heretic king," who became the successor to the throne upon the premature death of his older brother Tuthmosis, played no prominent role; he is mentioned only once, on a delivery for the *sed*-festival of his father.

The Search for New Intermediaries

The times were filled with a quest for a new closeness to the divine and for new intermediaries between the human and the divine realms. This is clear in the prominence of animal worship, the evidence for which increases under Amenophis III. The burials of the Apis bulls in the crypts at Saqqara began with him, and the crocodile sanctuary at el-Rizeiqat, south of Luxor, stems from his reign. There are also numerous monumental representations of animals, such as the baboons of Hermopolis and the scarab at Karnak, and there is also the sarcophagus for a cat dedicated by the crown prince Tuthmosis. In the minor arts, amuletic seals constantly depict the king as an animal: a lion, a sphinx, a bull, a falcon, or even a mongoose. Everything suggests that these are not popular trends now making their appearance at the official level, but rather that they represent an express policy of the royal court. Later, Akhenaten would deliberately steer a different course, just as he would counteract the tendency to the colossal.

The renewal that the sed-festival was supposed to effect was urgently needed, for the king was evidently seriously ill in his later years. This was known abroad, and his son-in-law Tushratta, the king of Mitanni, sent him a healing statue of the goddess Ishtar as a means to recovery. But the aged pharaoh set greater store by the Egyptian Sakhmet (Figure 2), the dangerous lion-headed goddess who was able to dispense illness as well as its cure. He had an apparent total of 730 (2 × 365) statues of the goddess set up in various temples at Thebes—a litany in stone, in which the mighty goddess was invoked in all her names and cultic forms to protect the king every day and every night of the year. He died before the third repetition of his sed-festival, and his son Amenophis IV, who would later style himself Akhenaten, began his rule.

The succession is closely bound up with the problem of a joint reign of the two rulers. Petrie was the first to think of a coregency of the new king with his father, since he found references to the elder king during his excavations at Amarna.

FIGURE 2. *Statue of the goddess Sakhmet from a temple of Amenophis III. Geneva, Musée d'Art et d'Histoire 20926 (Depositum from the Swiss Confederation). Gray granite, height 7'. Photo by Y. Siza, © Musée d'Art et d'Histoire.*

Such joint reigns of two royal partners were popular in the Middle Kingdom, for they brought a heightened stability to the Egyptian state. Use was made of this arrangement in the New Kingdom as well, especially in the case of Hatshepsut on behalf of her nephew Tuthmosis III, when he was still a minor, and the latter perhaps on behalf of his son Amenophis II. After 1951, when H. W. Fairman revived the idea of a coregency of Akhenaten in the third volume of his *City of Akhenaten,* attempting to support it with various pieces of circumstantial evidence, a number of authors followed him in this presumption. Cyril Aldred in particular continually championed a long, twelve-year coregency of the two rulers. Since this left only five years for Akhenaten's sole rule, this proposed coregency had far-reaching consequences, as we already indicated at the end of Chapter 1.

In recent years, no new, genuinely conclusive evidence for a coregency has emerged. A representation of Amenophis III on the Third Pylon at Karnak displays a sculptor's correction and is by no means the later erasure of a "coregent" depicted on a smaller scale—in fact, two coregents would have had to be of the same size! It can also be noted that the name of Amun is overall intact in the tomb of Amenophis III, while the hieratic docket on Amarna Letter 27 is to be read "year 2" and thus speaks to a direct succession. The only thing that can be maintained, after all this lengthy and intense debate, is that a long coregency of the two kings is untenable.

3

The First Steps

The Royal Titulary as Program for a Reign

The first thing we learn of Akhenaten after his ascent to the
throne is his titulary. In Egypt, this always represented a sort
of program for a reign, and, like a seismograph, it indicated
any change in the concept of kingship. In the case of the new
king, it is immediately striking that his original titulary
already contains no mention of the national god Amun, aside
from his personal name Amenophis. The usual foreign policy statements designating Pharaoh as triumphant over traditional enemies are absent, along with bellicose epithets.
Instead, we find a building program concentrated on Karnak:
"great of kingship in Karnak" (his *nebty* name) and "who
elevates the crowns in Thebes" (his Golden Horus name), as
well as the "god and ruler in Thebes" added to his personal
name, with "Thebes" meaning first and foremost the temple
complex of Karnak.

Pharaoh's Titulary

From the Middle Kingdom on, upon assuming the throne,
each Egyptian monarch adopted a detailed titulary consisting of five names, each of which was connected to one
of the standard titles. These were:

1. The *Horus name*, which designated Pharaoh as the manifestation of the old sky god Horus, as "Horus in the
   palace" (Horus as son of Osiris was considerably later!).
   This name was therefore written within a representation
   of the palace, a rectangular outline with a niched facade,
   atop which is perched the Horus-falcon. The earliest
   kings, around 3000 B.C.E., were designated only by this
   name. In the New Kingdom, the Horus name regularly
   began with the element "Mighty Bull," but was otherwise quite variable.

2. The *Nebty name*, referring to the "Two Ladies," Nekhbet
   and Wadjit, the protective goddesses of Upper and
   Lower Egypt respectively; they are concretely depicted
   as a vulture and a serpent, each atop a basket, the
   hieroglyphic sign for "lord, lady." The title alludes to the
   duality of Pharaoh's domain, as does the frequent title
   "Lord of the Two Lands." The "Two Ladies" correspond
   to the royal gods Horus and Seth, the "Two Lords."

3. The *Gold name* or *Golden Horus name* is mostly written
   with a falcon atop a beaded collar, the hieroglyphic sign
   for "gold," but the interpretation of the falcon as Horus
   is uncertain.

4. The *Throne name*, preceded by the title "King of Upper
   and Lower Egypt," is enclosed in a cartouche, a long
   oval that surrounds the throne name protectively, like
   an amulet. From the late Old Kingdom on, the throne
   name was compounded with the name of the sun god
   Re and thus included the hieroglyph of the sun disk. The
   name was once explained as a theological statement
   concerning the god, but in more recent scholarship, it
   is taken as a statement regarding the king.

5. The *Personal name*, which follows the title "Son of Re."
   This is the name the prince had been given at birth, but,

as king, he enclosed it in a cartouche, like the throne name. Each king thus had cartouches enclosing two of his names, for which reason Akhenaten also placed the "didactic" name of his god Aten in two cartouches. The personal names are mostly cited in the Greek forms that have come down to us, such as Amenophis or Tuthmosis.

This titulary remained in use down to the Roman emperors, who ruled Egypt as pharaohs, though they employed it in an abbreviated form. Seldom do all five elements of the titulary appear on a royal monument. When the king was referred to by only one name, the throne name was regularly employed.

For a collection of royal names from all periods, see Jürgen von Beckerath, Handbuch der ägyptischen Königsnamen, *Münchner ägyptologische Studien 20 (Munich and Berlin, 1984).*

There, at Karnak, arose the new king's first sanctuary. It was not dedicated, however, to the actual lord of the temple complex, Amun-Re, King of the Gods, but to the sun god. The latter was still represented with a falcon's head in the traditional manner, but in addition to Re-Harakhty he was also called Aten, a designation that had previously indicated the physical manifestation of the sun and only now enjoyed divine worship. Early inscriptions of the new king in the sandstone quarries of Gebel el-Silsila, where the blocks for Karnak were extracted, are concerned with the great construction project for Re-Harakhty-Aten. There, the king still appears before Amun-Re in the traditional manner, even though his building project was intended for Re-Harakhty.

Though the king is designated as the one "whom Amun-Re chose from among millions" on a scarab in the British

Museum, his reign clearly betrays, from its very beginning, a bias against this heretofore preeminent god. And while Egyptian kings normally endeavored to effectuate a comprehensive program for their reigns immediately upon ascending the throne, showing themselves to be creator gods by means of construction works and military campaigns, repelling enemies and "lighting" the world with their monuments, in the case of Akhenaten, we note curiously little activity aside from his building project at Karnak. One senses that he was expending all his energy on the formulation of his "teaching," his attempt to remodel the world.

The first results were soon apparent. The new god received a formal name, one such as no Egyptian deity had ever had, or ever would have again. He was called "Re-Harakhty, who rejoices in the horizon in his name Shu, who is Aten" (Figure 3). This was the older form of the so-called "didactic name," though it was really less a name than a sort of credo. The next step, apparently carried out in the third year of the king's reign, was to enclose the name in two cartouches, as though it were part of a royal titulary. Perhaps this step was taken on the occasion of the *sed*-festival that the god celebrated together with the king.

The Origin of a God

For the first time in history, we have a close-up view of how a deity originated. It is as though the Aten suddenly emerged from the traditional form of the sun god and then quickly shed the last vestiges of his origin. At the beginning, he conformed to the traditional, mixed form of a man with the falcon's head of the solar deity Re-Harakhty. The falcon-headed god was at first still used as a hieroglyph in the throne name of the king, and we can see that in general, the king preferred

FIGURE 3. *The royal couple, accompanied by three princesses, making a presentation of cartouches containing the earlier form of the didactic name of the Aten. After N. de G. Davies,* The Rock Tombs of El Amarna, *vol. 4, Memoirs of the Archaeological Survey of Egypt 16, pl. 31.*

the falcon as a tutelary power. From an altar to the sun at Karnak stems the first known representation of Pharaoh in the company of the solar baboons and the animal-headed powers of Buto and Hierakonpolis! Later, however, the theriomorphic aspect of deities was discredited; only the uraeus and the falcon continued to be tolerated, while the king remained a bull in his titulary (every pharaoh of the New Kingdom was a "mighty bull" in his Horus name).

The ever more dogmatic name of the god, which was enclosed in two cartouches, clearly followed the model of the royal titulary, which also entailed two cartouches. By the late Middle Kingdom, certain divine names could be highlighted by placing them in a cartouche, and in the New Kingdom, Amun-Re was styled "king of the gods," but until this time there had never been such a rigorous systematization of the royalty of a god.

The Sanctuaries at Karnak

We know rather little regarding the exact location of the Aten sanctuaries at Karnak. It is certain at least that the Gempaaten, with its colossal statues of the king (Figure 4), lay in the eastern part of the temple complex and was thus oriented toward the sunrise. One of the sanctuaries seems to have been entirely reserved for the chief royal wife, Nefertiti. Akhenaten was not represented there; rather, the queen was depicted, alone or with her daughters, carrying out cultic activities normally performed by the king, down to the presentation of Maat and the smiting of enemies. The queen also received a new name: Neferneferuaten, "Aten is the most perfect" (or, "most beautiful"). Though she was not provided with a throne name, the frequent doubling of her cartouche constituted a sort of substitute for one.

Nefertiti's religious role surpassed that of Teye. In group statues, she appears striding at the king's right, which was highly unusual for a queen. She assisted the king in all his cultic activities, even the smiting of enemies, and she herself was even depicted in this triumphal pose. In the avenue of sphinxes leading up to the temple of Karnak from the south, Akhenaten and Nefertiti originally alternated as sphinxes; later, Tutankhamun altered both into ram-headed sphinxes in honor of Amun.

From the very beginning, representations of the royal family stressed the intimacy that would be so characteristic of the art of the Amarna Period (Figure 5), and which would continue to appear in art under Tutankhamun. On blocks from an early Aten sanctuary there is a scene of Akhenaten being

FIGURE 4. *Colossal statue of Amenophis IV, originally from Karnak. Cairo Museum. Photo by Nancy J. Corbin.*

FIGURE 5. *Princess and nurse. Brooklyn Museum 37.405. Limestone, 11" × 4.5". Photo courtesy of the Brooklyn Museum.*

dressed, and the royal couple even appear in front of their conjugal bed in the palace while the Aten, with his hands outstretched in blessing, shines down upon them.

The name Gempaaten is also a sign of the linguistic reform to come, for it already contains the definite article of Late Egyptian. Akhenaten elevated the spoken language of the New Kingdom, which we call Late Egyptian, into a new written language. It was supposed to replace Middle Egyptian, which had developed at the end of the Old Kingdom. This reform outlasted Akhenaten, and a rich Late Egyptian literature developed soon after his reign, though Middle Egyptian remained the language of religious texts and official royal inscriptions.

At the outset of the reign, relatively large blocks were used in the sun temple of Re-Harakhty, but later the new sanctuaries of the Aten were erected from small, easily carried sandstone blocks called *talatat* ("three"-blocks) in the scholarly literature because they are one handbreadth in height and two in width. Isolated blocks were already visible in the vicinity of the temples of Karnak and Luxor in the nineteenth century, but since the beginning of the twentieth, extensive restoration efforts by French and Egyptian Egyptologists have recovered such *talatat* by the tens of thousands from a great variety of structural elements. Besides the temple complex of Karnak, the temples of Luxor, Tod, Nag el-Madamud, and Armant have yielded up still more blocks. Together with those still in the Tenth Pylon at Karnak, we must reckon with more than fifty thousand decorated blocks that once constituted whole temple walls: a gigantic jigsaw puzzle to be reconstructed into scenes of the cult! There was an early attempt to do this by computer, but the results were rather disappointing. Since 1965, when Ray Smith took on the project, only a small selection has been published, and these are marked by dubious combinations and reconstructions. Still, work on the blocks has brought to light a host of iconographic treasures that enrich our knowledge of the early years of Akhenaten. Here, we can make use of a series of photographs taken by Ursula Schweitzer (Figures 6 and 7) prior to 1960, when the blocks were still lying outdoors at Karnak before being put into storehouses.

Once Again, the *Sed*-Festival

On these blocks, an important role is played by the *sed*-festival that Akhenaten celebrated together with his god Aten. We have already mentioned this festival of royal renewal in the previous chapter, in connection with its celebration by Amenophis III. But while the father endeavored to gather all the deities of the land for this festival and to perform its ceremonies in front of shrines containing various divine images, his son strode from one shrine to another, each containing only the Aten, depicted as the sun disk with its rays. Along with traditional motifs like the dances for Hathor, there are novel and unusual scenes; one depicts the king with a hammer in his hand.

FIGURE 6. Talatat-*blocks from the temple of Karnak. Photos by U. Schweitzer.*

FIGURE 7. Talatat-*blocks from the temple of Karnak. Photos by
U. Schweitzer.*

The representation of the festival cannot itself attest to its celebration, for the Egyptians always created reality through pictures alone. Even Akhenaten had himself and Nefertiti represented as felling enemies without having undertaken a military campaign. Yet there is some reason to think that Akhenaten inaugurated the royal status of his god Aten with the celebration of a *sed*-festival. Whether he celebrated his own thirtieth birthday at the same time, as some have supposed, remains highly uncertain.

Though the king planned for "millions" of *sed*-festivals in the text of the earlier boundary stelae of his new capital and obliged himself to celebrate them there and nowhere else, he evidently did not celebrate any festival of renewal at Akhetaten; at the least, there is no evidence for one. An actual *sed*-festival should have left traces in a great number of inscriptions preserved on vessels. Instead, there is only a single wish for the celebration of *sed*-festivals, carved on a door frame from the house of the officer Nekhuenpaaten.

The Grotesque Pharaoh

The reliefs carved on the *talatat* and the colossal statues in the Gempaaten temple are the earliest evidence for the realization of an entirely new artistic style on Akhenaten's part. Heinrich Schäfer described the impression it makes on modern beholders in the following words in 1931: "Anyone who steps in front of certain of these representations for the first time recoils from this epitome of physical repulsiveness. His head seems to float atop his long, thin neck. His chest is sunken, yet there is something feminine about its form. Below his bloated paunch and his fat thighs, his skinny calves are a match for his spindly arms. His face is deeply lined, and he has a sharply receding forehead and a weak chin."

As we saw above, Champollion had already employed the term *morbidezza* (softness). According to Alfred Wiedemann, these representations of the king "in a frightfully ugly form, with distorted features and a pendulous belly, are a complete caricature." Walther Wolf invoked "sick ugliness and nervous decadence" in reference to the colossal statues at Karnak, and many others have echoed this theme of caricature. Naturally enough, modern writers have assumed that the contemporaries of the king shared the horror that Schäfer conjures up, and many have felt that Akhenaten wanted to shock, setting his repulsive ugliness (Figure 8) in deliberate contrast to the beauty of the traditional art. We shall not enter into a stylistic analysis of Amarna art here, but rather lay stress on some criteria that can yield, over and above his artistic taste, an insight into the overall mentality of this reformer.

The repose to which we are accustomed in Egyptian sculpture is here set aside in a manner that can even be called frightful; movement, expression, emotion, and disregard for reality are now the rule. The essence of this art, which was at first designated despairingly as merely "ugly" or even "sick," can be understood by comparing it with schools of modern art that deal

FIGURE 8. *Akhenaten (sculptor's trial piece). Berlin 14512. Limestone, 5 ⅞" × 5 ¼". Photo by M. Büsing, Ägyptisches Museum und Papyrussammlung SMB.*

freely with the human form. As early as 1926, Schäfer called Amarna art "expressionistic," as did Alexander Scharff, and it is doubtless more apt to employ this designation than to speak of "realism," on the assumption that Akhenaten actually looked like his depictions. This art is a manneristic distortion of reality, a rebellion against the classical ideal of beauty established earlier in Dynasty 18.

Everything that had been static, fixed in place for eternity, is now set in motion. Vertical axes become diagonal, stressed by receding foreheads and elongated crowns. The contours of the human figure swell and recede, creating the rhythmic play of the overly swollen thighs and the scrawny, "chicken-like" calves (as Thomas Mann called them), and even the chin and lips are swollen. We also encounter new motion in the king's encounters with his god, with the offerings raised on high meeting the rays beaming down from the solar disk. And, finally, movement characterizes the playful, caressing intimacy of the royal family, which is depicted in lively group scenes, and the fluttering bands of cloth that dangle from clothes, crowns, and articles of furniture.

Akhenaten introduced the chariot drawn by a pair of horses as a means of expressing this new motion (Figure 9), and he might well have intended it to imitate the swift course of his god across the sky. In no other period did Egyptian art contain so many representations of chariots, and no longer just in battle or the hunt, but as the means of rapid transportation evidently employed by the king on a regular basis; only in the temple did he still tread respectfully. An ecstasy of speed pervades the chariot scenes. On one of the blocks from Hermopolis, a team of horses races into an enormous open space; nothing halts their rapid movement, and one of the horses turns its head, resulting in a rare frontal view (Figure 10).

FIGURE 9. *The royal couple in a chariot. After N. de G. Davies,* The Rock Tombs of El Amarna, *vol. 3, Memoirs of the Archaeological Survey of Egypt 15, pl. 32A.*

FIGURE 10. *Detail, chariot scene. Brooklyn Museum 60.28. Limestone, 21" × 9". Photo courtesy of the Brooklyn Museum.*

This movement also characterizes the representations of *proskynesis* so popular at this time; like the faithful praying in a mosque, whole rows of officials bow down to the ground in prayerful adoration of the king, just as Akhenaten is from time to time depicted lying outstretched on the ground before his god. The upper part of a stela from Hermopolis depicts the royal family on their knees beneath the radiant Aten, while in the lower part, they are lying flat on the ground, "kissing the earth," as the Egyptians put it.

No Fear of Emotion

Along with movement, there is emotion: the obligatory kissing, embracing, and caressing among the royal family, the mourning of the royal couple at the bier of their daughter Meketaten, Nefertiti as a nursing mother, and all the scenes of intimacy that occur only in the art of Amarna. All these are intended to depict how the love that emanated from Aten determined the togetherness of his creatures, as exemplified in Pharaoh's immediate surroundings. And with that, any inhibition against depicting and emphasizing emotion has vanished.

A breath of previously unknown freedom seems to blow through this art, and one has the feeling that the artists must have done their work free of all former conventions. But this is only one aspect, which was complemented by a strong commitment to principles newly established by Akhenaten as obligatory. Even the "expressionism" of this art does not signify freedom, but rather represents a binding obligation. It is constantly stressed in the texts that the king himself established the guidelines for artistic production.

Akhenaten did not shy from questioning even the basic principles of Egyptian art. His artists tried their hand at bold turns and frontal views, and on the reconstructed temple wall in the Luxor Museum (Figure 11) it can be seen how even the convention of scale was no longer binding; in the two lower registers, the king making offerings in the temple is depicted as smaller in size than the men walking to the temple behind him carrying offerings and cult implements! This entails the annulment of a strict rule that had determined pictorial composition since the beginnings of Egyptian art: the size of the individuals represented, whether deities, humans, or animals, did not depend on the accident of their appearance, but on their relative importance within the scene. Akhenaten's artists otherwise adhered to this principle, especially in representing the royal family.

FIGURE 11. *Reconstructed temple wall of Akhenaten. Luxor Museum. Photo by E. Krüger.*

Only One God

Aten's coexistence with the other deities lasted for only a short time. The traditional divine multiplicity was still fully present at the king's *sed*-festival, for their temples and domains were obliged to contribute to the financing of the great festival and the new construction projects; the exclusivity of the Aten was thus at first only a relative one—like many an Egyptian deity, he was *unique* but not *exclusive*. But in the representations, only the radiant Aten appears in the divine chapels of the *sed*-festival, while in a highly fragmentary inscription from the Ninth Pylon which reproduces a speech by the king, the new god is emphatically contrasted to the other deities. In the Theban tomb of Parennefer (who was still "overseer of the prophets of all the gods"!) a text stresses that "one measures the payments to every (other) god with a level measure, but for the Aten one measures so that it overflows"—this in contrast to the warning in the popular "Story of the Eloquent Peasant" not to fill to overflowing, or not to overdo Maat, as the sage Ptahhotpe had quite similarly advised.

In the future, the Aten with his rays would be the only permissible icon of the god. The mixed form of a human body and an animal's head would vanish, and only the hands emanating from the sun would serve as a reminder of his former human form. At an early stage, these hands could still hold any sort of object; thus, in smiting scenes, they even held weapons that they extended to Pharaoh! In connection with the *sed*-festival, they held the hieroglyph designating this festival by way of a wish for many repetitions of it. But in the final form of the "radiant Aten" only the *ankh* sign, the hieroglyph for "life," remained, extended to the noses of the king and the queen. The rays depicted in the art are mentioned again and again in the hymns to the Aten as a token of the proximity of this "distant" god.

Akhenaten's "Perestroika"

From the third to the fifth year of his reign, Akhenaten carried out a "perestroika" that affected every area of life and which cannot be compared to any other phase in Egyptian history. The vast extent of the reorganization was unique— religion, art, language, and literature were affected, and surely also the administration and the economy, for a little later the temples of the traditional deities would be closed and their priests dismissed from state service or "reindoctrinated." But there was no persecution at this time, though in year 4 the high priest of Amun was sent literally "into the desert" on a quarrying expedition. Only a few weeks before the founding of the new Residence, the administrator Ipi reported to the king from Memphis that all was in order in the temple of Ptah and that all the deities were receiving their prescribed offerings.

Though his measures were considered and gradual, there was certainly opposition. In the text of his boundary stelae, the king himself speaks of "bad things" he had heard in his fourth and preceding regnal years, though without identifying the opposition by name; in the highly damaged continuation of the text, he seems to be precluding future opposition. Indicative is the military presence that we encounter already on the Theban *talatat* and then later in the rock-cut tombs at Amarna. Scurrying soldiers, predominantly a guard of Asiatics and blacks, surround the king and prevent any resistance. Indeed, Akhenaten was the only founder of a religion to have all the instruments of state power at his disposal, and we should assume that he employed them ruthlessly to realize his ideas. Only underground opposition was possible, and "lamentations" gave expression to a widespread sentiment among the common people and the former elite.

It cannot be said how widespread approval of the reorganization was, but it probably was not crucial for the reformer's further course. His next step brought a new royal titulary, from which were removed not only the name of the hated Amun but also references to his locales of Thebes and Karnak; in his new *nebty* name, Karnak was replaced by the newly founded Residence of Akhetaten. Akhenaten could keep his former throne name *Neferkheprure,* just as he remained "the sole one of Re" (*Waenre*), but he changed his personal name Amenophis into the name by which the world today knows him, and which in Egyptian sounded something like *Akhanyati*—"He who is useful to Aten," or perhaps "Radiance of Aten"; the rendering "Soul of Aten" is less suitable because *akh* actually denotes only the soul of a deceased person, while Akhenaten's formulation "I am your son who is useful to you and elevates your name" speaks in favor of the meaning "to be useful." The exact nuance of the name escapes us, and in this volume we employ the conventional form Akhenaten rather than the more accurate Akhanyati—the precise vocalization of ancient Egyptian is problematic, since the hieroglyphic writing system did not indicate the vowels.

"The Beautiful Child of the Living Aten"

The traditional titles of Pharaoh remained unaltered, but the king was often pleased to style himself the "beautiful child of the living Aten"; representations of the king as a child were popular at this time and also served as amulets, replacements for the proscribed divine amulets of prior times. The Aten,

Akhenaten's god, did not change his own royal titulary until some years later.

The assumption of the new titulary coincided with the solemn foundation of a new Residence; both occurred in the fifth regnal year. Akhenaten finally decided no longer to adorn Thebes with temples for his new god Aten, and he sought out a place where he would not be hampered by monuments constructed in the traditional style or dedicated to the traditional deities. He found this place in a remote locale in Middle Egypt, where he would not be obliged to destroy anything but could simply build.

In moving the royal Residence, he could find a precedent in Amenemhet I, who inaugurated Dynasty 12 in the twentieth century B.C.E. and abandoned Thebes to found a new Residence just over thirty-seven miles south of Cairo, near the modern town of el-Lisht. But this was done solely for political reasons, not religious ones, whereas here the move was above all a religiously motivated *hegira* on the part of the religious reformer, one that did not take him to any of the old centers, but to this remote locale.

Before we have a look at Akhenaten's new Residence, we shall summarize the new teaching he promulgated, at least in its outlines.

4

A New Religion

No Divine Revelation

Akhenaten left no holy scripture, so what he founded does not belong to the religions of the book. And a "Word of God" is altogether inconceivable in this new religion, for the newly promulgated god remained silent. The Aten himself did not speak; rather, his preacher Akhenaten spoke about him. We must thus rely on evidence stemming from the inscriptions of the king and his officials.

The inscriptions frequently mention a "teaching" or "instruction" of Akhenaten's, which he placed in the hearts of his subjects. To be sure, the Egyptian word used for it, *sebayt*, also designates the wisdom literature handed down in writing from as early as the late Old Kingdom, but in the Amarna Period it seems in fact to be exclusively a matter of a teaching and instruction imparted orally by the king; nowhere is there a trace of religious tractates.

For a monarch of the New Kingdom, it is astonishing how little Akhenaten has left to us in writing: the boundary stelae of his new Residence with their two different texts, the "Great Hymn to the Aten," which has been ascribed to him—probably correctly, though it is recorded in the tomb of Aya—and a victory stela in distant Nubia, which was undoubtedly erected in the king's name by his viceroy there. Additionally, there are a few inscriptions from the beginning of his reign, and further hymns. Thus, for written sources regarding Akhenaten's religion we can only consult certain illuminating passages from the tomb inscriptions of his officials.

It speaks to the clarity and simplicity of this religion that such meager sources nevertheless yield a general picture, allowing us to gain some familiarity with its essential characteristics. But there is also pictorial evidence: representations of the god Aten and the royal family, and lavish depictions of architecture and other motifs in the tombs of officials, which furnish us with an insight into temples and palaces. Akhenaten endeavored to promulgate his teaching through mnemonic images, especially the sun disk with its rays but also scenes of his family. These motifs were stipulated and obligatory, leaving the artists little latitude, but the abundance of new pictorial motifs must have aroused a feeling that anything could be expressed figuratively. This continued to have an effect long after Akhenaten; an unprecedented wealth of religious images was developed during the Ramesside Period and later in Dynasty 21.

New was the compulsory nature of the pictures and the divine names of the Amarna Period. Previously, a considerable freedom prevailed in the designation of deities with names and epithets in a cult scene; it was even a principle to seek a lively variety, with as little repetition as possible. There was also leeway in the representation of deities and the constellations into which they were inserted. Indeed, each divinity had a multiplicity of names, forms of manifestation, and constellations to be taken into account. But now there was only *one* fixed name and *one* fixed image of the Aten; all variation was excluded, and even his epithets were reduced to a few stereotypes.

God as Pharaoh

We have already indicated the rigor with which the royal status of the god was now promulgated. Aten ruled the world as king, he had a royal titulary and wore the royal uraeus, and he even celebrated royal festivals of renewal. Just as officials often placed the name of their king on their statues, so now statues of the royal couple bore the cartouches of their king and god. And his universal rule was indicated pictorially by the many hands of the god, to which everything was accessible. After earlier, tentative attempts to provide the sun disk with hands, the perfected, brilliantly simple image of the radiant Aten was developed in a single, bold step. But the decided, plastic bulge the disk often displays (Figure 12) should not lead us to interpret it as a solar orb.

The Aten was actually not the sun disk, but rather the *light* that is in the sun and which, radiating from it, calls the world to life and keeps it alive. Heinrich Brugsch already emphasized that Aten was a god of light, and Jan Assmann has managed a fresh distillation of this view. Indeed, from

FIGURE 12. *Akhenaten as sphinx. Geneva, Musée d'Art et d'Histoire 27804. Limestone, 40"× 21". Photo courtesy of Musée d'Art et d'Histoire.*

early times, the sun with its rays had served in the writing system as a hieroglyph in writing words meaning "to shine" and the like.

In contrast to the rich mythic frameworks in which Egyptian deities had otherwise been embedded, the Aten remained free of such connections and constellations. In fact, it was said of him only that he ever and again creates the world and maintains it in life; but there was no longer an interest in the original creation of the world—Aten, "who built himself with his own hands," creates the world continually. The nightly journey through the netherworld and the defeat of Apopis, the enemy of the sun, were now gone; there is even no mention of the barque of the god, the vehicle of the sun's course (in Egypt, with its innumerable waterways, all deities traveled by boat!).

Pharaoh as God

Aten (or Re-Harakhty) was the god of Akhenaten, but the personal god of the individual was the king—as Assmann has put it, "He was the god who set out on procession, who performed signs and wonders, and who intervened in the destiny of the individual, holding life and death in his hands." The officials at Akhenaten's court cultivated the topos of total dependence, in which themes from the "loyalist instructions" of the Middle Kingdom were continued and expanded. The king was appealed to as the dispenser of all sustenance, and the epithets of a creator god were heaped on him; the mayor of the new capital conjured up the formula "Neferkheprure brings into being" as a new name for himself.

This position vis-à-vis humankind was not simply the traditional role of a pharaoh; rather, it had its origin in the status of Akhenaten as the beloved son of the Aten. Previously, Pharaoh had considered himself to be the "son of Re," thus stressing his divine origin. But Akhenaten was the son of his god in a much more personal manner, and in this lay the seed of the failure of his teaching, for it stood and fell along with his own person. For Egyptian theologians there also arose the question of the *homoousia* of father and son. In the eighth scene of the Book of Gates, a new description of the netherworld that originated in the Amarna Period (before or after Akhenaten), Atum expresses his total unity with Re with the formulation "I am the son who emerged from his father, I am the father who emerged from his son," at the same time alluding, in context, to the father-son relationship of Osiris and Horus.

While Aten was not just a national deity but rather illuminated the entire world as the universal sun god, Akhenaten always remained pharaoh of Egypt and never became a prophet for all humankind. On a purely superficial level, this is shown by his titulary: Akhenaten was "lord of the Two Lands," that is, Egypt, while the Aten was lord of the world, expressed concretely as "sky and earth."

Personal piety at this time consisted exclusively in loyalty to the king, which meant to Akhenaten as a person; no other intermediary was conceivable. We have already made reference to the excessive appeals made by his officials; veritable hymns were sung to him, as by Panehsy:

Praise to you, oh my god, who built me,
who determined good for me,
who made me come into being and gave me bread,
who cared for me with his ka!

. . . .

I give praise to the height of the heavens,
I adore the lord of the Two Lands, Akhenaten:
god of fate, giver of life, lord of command,

light of every land,
on whose gaze one lives.
Nile of humankind,
on whose ka one is sated.
God who creates the great ones and builds
   the poor ones,
breath for every nose, by which one breathes!

Akhenaten is constantly designated the Nile of Egypt, embodying the annual inundation and all the beneficence of nature, and he is also called "mother who bears all, he nourishes millions with his food," just as prior to Akhenaten, in the hymn of Suti and Hor, the sun god Re was designated "mother of humans and deities," while he would later often be called "mother and father."

The Female Element: Nefertiti

Akhenaten and his god thus partly accounted for the female sphere, but the third party in the alliance was Nefertiti, whose importance was already noted in the preceding chapter. This importance was not of a political but of a purely religious nature and thus had a different stress than in the case of Teye. Nefertiti shared in the rulership without being formally a coregent. She was Akhenaten's personal goddess, and she, along with him and the Aten, comprised a divine trinity, like those which so often occur in the pantheon of the New Kingdom. The constellation that shines through here is that of Atum, the single god at the beginning of creation, and the pair Shu and Tefenet who emerged from him. This is quite clear at the beginning of the reign, when, for example, some of the colossal statues of Akhenaten wear the four-feathered crown of Shu. Later, the indications became more recondite, as when the royal couple "elevate" the names of the Aten.

Possible Advisers

The question must be posed whether, aside from the royal couple, any other persons took part in developing this new religion. Nowhere does Akhenaten name anyone to whom he felt indebted; rather, he constantly stresses that he alone knows the Aten. The oft stressed influence of Heliopolis, the old religious center of the solar cult, on the new beliefs regarding the Aten cannot be substantiated; the high priest there, Anen, a brother of Teye, was certainly among the dignitaries whom the young prince often encountered at court, but we know nothing about his religious conceptions or his possible influence. Nor do the sources reveal anything about the religious leanings of Teye, the king's mother, much as one might care to ascribe a certain influence to her.

Among all the officials at the court of his father, a man named Amenhotpe stands out. Distinct from the many other men of this name, which even Akhenaten bore at first, he was called "Amenhotpe son of Hapu" (Figure 13) and came from Athribis in the delta. Provided with the title "scribe of recruits," one that was not especially high, he was presented by his king with distinctly unusual tokens of royal grace; thus he was the only official of the New Kingdom to receive a mortuary temple of his own on the west bank of Thebes, which was an otherwise exclusively royal prerogative. He is portrayed as a wise scribe in a series of statues from Karnak, and in the Late Period he was revered as a deified sage; he tended to be mentioned in the same breath as Imhotep, the architect of the first pyramid. Amenhotpe also directed important construction projects for his monarch, such as the transport and erection of the Colossi of Memnon; at an advanced age he also supervised Pharaoh's *sed*-festival. Hapu's son must thus have been an unusual and outstanding personality, one who lived on in the memory of the people,

FIGURE 13. *Amenhotpe, son of Hapu, depicted as a scribe. Cairo Museum J. 44861. Gray granite, height 50 ⅜". Photo by H. Hauser.*

and who quite likely also made an impression on the successor to the throne as he was growing up. But no source informs us of what Akhenaten materially owed him.

At the end of the reign of Amenophis III, the two viziers Ramose and Aper-El stood nominally at the head of the administration, but there is no indication that they pursued any particular religious line. The change from the traditional to the new artistic style, with the royal couple under the sun disk with its rays, is documented in the Theban tomb (TT 55) of Ramose; he thus supported the reform outwardly, but he must have died soon thereafter. Next to the viziers, the Viceroy of Nubia ("Kush"), who at this time was Merymes, had a prominent position because of his office.

Aya certainly had considerable influence. He was evidently a brother of Teye, and also tutor to and perhaps even father-in-law of Akhenaten, if Nefertiti actually came from this prominent family from Akhmim. Aya played an important role during the entire Amarna Period; the king's "Great Hymn to the Aten" is recorded in his tomb, and it is highly tempting to understand him as a sort of guru of the young reformer. But it must be stressed in this case as well that no secure sources for this have yet been found.

The remaining officials of the time remain mere names, their personalities unknown to us. But there was undoubtedly a circle of officials at court who were loyally devoted to the new king and his religious teaching. For this clique consisting of the king and his officials, it was now necessary to find a new place, one unencumbered by the burden of tradition and the proximity of the old deities, and free of witnesses to the past—a virgin territory in every respect.

5

A City for a God

The Founding of Akhetaten

First, Akhenaten set up boundary stelae (Figure 14) around the place he had chosen for his future royal Residence so as to delineate its intended area with due solemnity. The fourteen stelae—three on the west bank of the Nile and eleven on the east bank—staked out an extensive area, though the actual city would lie only on the eastern bank, where the cemeteries are also to be found. The "beautiful West," up to then the realm of the dead, would no longer play a role.

The date on the three earlier stelae can be reconstructed as the thirteenth day of the fourth month of the season *peret* in the fifth regnal year of the king. It thus falls only one brief month after that of a letter sent from Memphis by the administrator Ipi, a nephew of the vizier Ramose, to the king, who was probably already encamped at Amarna. In this letter, Ipi informs the monarch, who was still called Amenophis, that all was well in the temple of Ptah at Memphis and that the prescribed offerings were being carried out in their entirety for all the gods and goddesses of Memphis, with nothing being withheld from them. All this was being done in the name of the king, and Ipi designated the king's relationship to the god Ptah as "your true father, from whom you emerged."

FIGURE 14. *Representation on Akhetaten boundary stela S. After N. de G. Davies,* The Rock Tombs of El Amarna, *vol. 5, Memoirs of the Archaeological Survey of Egypt 17, pl. 26.*

We owe a scenario for the founding of the new capital to the American astronomer Ronald Wells, who has studied the orientation of Egyptian temples. According to him, the date chosen was that on which, for an observer, the rising sun shone directly into the length of the small temple, that is, the mortuary temple of the king, from an indentation in the eastern horizon where the desert valley that was to contain the royal tomb opened up into the broad plain of Amarna; around 1350 B.C.E., this day was March 4 in the Julian calendar, or February 20 in the Gregorian calendar. It well suited Akhenaten's religion of light that the foundation date occurred when the Aten emerged from the valley that the king had earmarked for his own and his family's tomb, flooding with his light the plain where the city was to lie. Wells's assumption is thus attractive, but it has also found objections: the temple axis has in no way been established that exactly, nor is it clear just how sunrise was defined in those ancient times. Still, the very name of the new Residence, Akhetaten—"Horizon (or, Place of the Light) of Aten"—is programmatic, referring to the sun as a heavenly body.

The remaining boundary stelae are dated exactly a year later, on the same date in year 6; three of them delineate a broad district on the west bank of the Nile, though nothing was ever built on it. The entire extended district was solemnly dedicated to the new god, "with (its) hills, deserts, fields, and towns, with (its) people, animals, and vegetation," as the text of the stelae puts it. This presentation to the god was reinforced by a solemn oath that the king swore by the life of the Aten, and also by that of his wife and his children. He dedicated the new capital to the Aten "as a monument to his name for all time"—thanks to divine inspiration, for the god himself had shown him this place that fulfilled his ideal requirements. No god and no goddess, no ruler of olden times, could lay claim to this place, which was entirely unspoiled, a pure environment for the rays of the Aten.

This was a place where the Aten and his beloved son and preacher could rule alone, where its inhabitants could devote themselves entirely to the service of the pharaoh and his god, unburdened by any traces of the past. Here, the perfect realization of the new religion was at last possible; in the years that followed, it would become ever purer, but also ever more extreme. We shall turn to the mature form of the teaching in the next chapter.

The desert terrace on the east bank, crisscrossed by a few shallow depressions, offered a site well suited to the intended metropolis. First, a camp was set up, as noted in the later text of the stelae of year 6; from there, the king was able to inspect the construction work when he visited. The work progressed quickly—the repetition of the king's oath in his eighth regnal year might indicate the court's move to the new Residence at that early date. We must imagine a gigantic construction site already in year 5, and this was the year when the regular deliveries of wine to the Aten's city commenced. In year 6, Amun's domains in the delta still participated in the supply.

An Unusual Residence

The new city, which was literally built from the ground up—for a great many unbaked mud bricks were used, even in official buildings—was no ordinary royal Residence, but rather a cult place devoted to the service of Aten, his prophet Akhenaten, and the latter's family (Figure 15). The rock tombs of the higher officials and the inscribed entrances of their dwellings tell us who made their fixed abode here under the king's spell. They were the personnel of the Aten sanctuary, with its high priest Meryre and the administrator and overseer of cattle at their head; the overseer of the palace and the overseer of the harem; the personal physician of the king; the mayor and the administration of the new city; temple scribes and officials of the treasury; architects and artists; officers and police officials. One very important man was the police chief Mahu, whose tomb decoration contains scenes from his professional life; such scenes were otherwise no longer usual in the tombs at Amarna, where the officials receded behind the representation of the royal family, upon whom salvation in the afterlife now depended.

Among the officials at Akhetaten, we find one of the viziers, but none of the other heads of the civil administration and, naturally, no priests aside from those who served the god Aten and his prophet Akhenaten. The new Residence was evidently not intended to be the seat of the administration of the land. That remained in Memphis, where a great

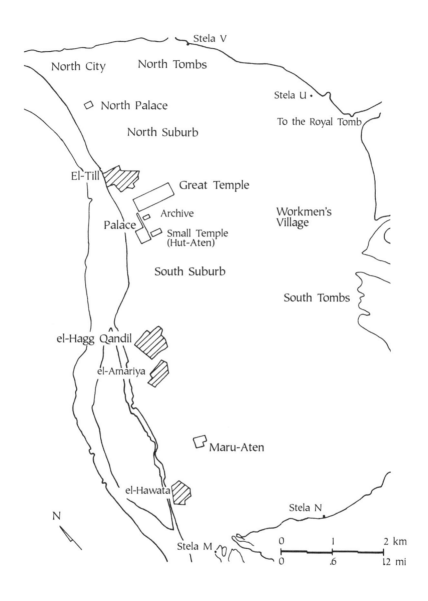

FIGURE 15. *Plan of Akhetaten. Prepared from various sources by G. Roulin.*

deal of it had already been transferred, under Akhenaten's predecessors, from the somewhat remote Thebes. Notwithstanding the open location of the new city, which made do without walls, access was evidently barred to unauthorized persons. No social underclass made its appearance in the cityscape; servants and slaves had no houses of their own, but rather were integrated into the households of their masters, the royal followers. And an urban proletariat could not have developed very quickly in this place where all inhabitants had their set function. We can thus expect no poor neighborhood in what Joachim Spiegel has called this "city of villas and palaces."

The layout of the new Residence was also unusual. To the north and the south, sections filled with villas—in no way typical for an ancient Egyptian city—surrounded an "official" center containing a palace, temples, barracks, government bureaus, storehouses, archives, and so forth. There was no set quarter for workshops, for these were associated with individual households. Shops, taverns, and schools have left no architectural traces; the last are evidently to be sought in the temple area. A street life, such as might be expected in southerly climes, could not have developed here. The main street, more than thirty feet wide and running parallel to the Nile, served principally for the daily chariot trip by the king and his retinue from his palace in the north to the cult buildings in the city center, a journey several miles long. We have already mentioned that Akhenaten was the first pharaoh to discover the chariot drawn by a pair of horses as a means of rapid locomotion and of royal representation. Previously, only depictions of battles and hunts contained chariots, with which the Egyptians had become familiar only in the New Kingdom. Now, Akhenaten used it at every opportunity as an expression of the movement that also characterized the new artistic style of this period. The inhabitants of the city probably experienced Pharaoh for the most part in the cloud of dust from his train of chariots.

According to a plausible estimate, the entire population must have amounted to between fifty and one hundred thousand inhabitants. A hierarchy of dwellings can be reconstructed from the preserved ground plans uncovered by the excavators. The high officials valued show. Their homesteads had entrances that even teams of horses could use, for, when possible, they copied the royal model of travel by chariot. One of the higher officials of the Residence, named Any, even had himself immortalized on his tomb stela with his team and his charioteer, Tjay. Additionally the titles and names of the owners would be displayed at the entrance to their homes, chiseled permanently in stone, a practice otherwise usual only in tombs. The dwellings (Figure 16) of these great lords contained as many as twenty rooms, grouped around a central columned hall; there were also a courtyard and working quarters such as stables, storehouses, and workshops, and, when possible, a private garden, a conspicuous luxury in this poorly watered region.

Comfort Is Required

Even middle-sized homes had, on average, a floor area of nearly forty square yards and contained a number of rooms, and we must remember that the flat roofs would also have been used. Many of the houses had baths and toilets, and often they also had a fountain of their own and a cult chapel for the worship of an image of the king and his family under the sun disk with its rays. The rank of a household can also be gauged by the thickness of its walls, which, along with its openings, served to control the climate within. More than

FIGURE 16. *The old German House at Thebes, built in 1926 by L. Borchardt in the style of a villa at Amarna. Photo by E. Hornung.*

half the houses had thin walls only half a brick thick; the walls of the remainder were up to three bricks in thickness, maintaining maximum protection against heat and cold. There was also an attempt to surround the central living area on all sides with as many subsidiary rooms as possible, so as to equalize climatic fluctuations to the extent feasible. The political and religious leadership lived in these better homes, along with their immediate assistants, while the simpler dwellings belonged to that larger, lower social class who carried out all the many tasks that had to be performed in such a place.

The neighborhoods where the officials lived were restricted to the proximity of the Nile, which served as both a highway and a source of water. The water supply must also have served the private and public gardens that characterized this cityscape. The king sought to integrate his palace to the north of the city completely into the world of nature by means of gardens and murals. Moreover, representations and elaborate stalls testify to a sort of "zoological garden" filled with wild desert animals, which Akhenaten could here observe at close range so as to rejoice at his god's care for all his creatures. This garden, incidentally, was not an innovation, for a zoo with the most exotic animals possible—these made their appearance in the tribute from foreign lands—had already in earlier times formed a part of Pharaoh's claim to universal sovereignty as far as the borders of the ordered world.

Akhetaten covered a strip of land not quite two-thirds of a mile wide, while its north-south axis, which followed the course of the river, amounted to over two miles in length, or more than five and a half miles including its outlying districts. This area was built on very sparsely, which was highly unusual for a Near Eastern city; there was thus plenty of room left to be filled by a future increase in the city's population.

Further to the east, and already in the midst of the desert, was a workmen's settlement that is supposed to have taken the place of the village of Deir el-Medina at Thebes; it is possible that the Theban specialists who had previously worked on the royal and private tombs on the west bank were resettled here en masse. While the Residence itself did not have city walls, here a wall surrounded the core of densely packed houses, though they were only seventy in number. The settlement had to be supplied with water from outside, and the British excavations were able to ascertain traces of extensive raising of pigs, with which the villagers supported themselves in addition to the provisions they received from the state. Though the pig could be considered an unclean animal in ancient Egypt, it was definitely used economically, and it also served to remove waste. Visitors to the capital would thus encounter on its streets not only the royal couple and their entourage but also herds of swine with their drovers!

The officials in the Residence were paid their salaries in the form of grain, as indicated by the large silos and the ovens in their homes. They were able to use some of it to pay their domestic servants and also to exchange it for other necessary goods. We may assume, moreover, that they shared in the food that was laid out daily for the god Aten on the innumerable altars of his temple and which was surely cleared away again at the end of the ceremonies. In most of the preserved sources, payments are calculated in bread and beer, the most important natural products; in Egypt, coinage developed only in the Late Period, as a means of paying Greek mercenaries.

The City of Light

Akhetaten was a city for Aten, the god of the light that emanated from the sun and, in Akhenaten's view, gave life to the world. To express this concept, he coined the ingenious, simple image of the sun disk with its rays and its many hands. So that these divine hands might everywhere have unhindered access, the altars in his temple precinct were set up under the open sky, while the king's processional way into the temple suffered no roof over itself, guaranteeing his constant contact with the deity and his visible image, the sun. There were thus no shadowy columned halls or dark interior rooms, as in traditional temples.

In Egypt's climate, this was an innovation that made an unreasonable demand on Akhenaten's entourage. Perhaps a sunshade was held over the king and his consort, but his entourage received no such favor. The diplomatic correspondence (Amarna Letter 16) preserves a complaint by the Assyrian king Assuruballit that his ambassadors were obliged to wait under the blazing sun until Pharaoh lent them his ear—"they are letting them die under the sun!" This shows to what an extreme the new belief in the omnipotence of light promulgated by Akhenaten determined life in this city.

At an earlier date, the royal oath on the boundary stelae was interpreted by scholars to mean that Akhenaten intended never to leave his new Residence. This does not emerge from the text, and Akhenaten even gives express instructions in case of his absence from the city; but the king undoubtedly preferred to stay in Akhetaten, working on the further development of his teaching, whose later form we shall treat in the next chapter. Art also underwent further development. While the representations on the boundary stelae still paid homage to the extreme early style of Amarna art, a less severe, more mature style quickly asserted itself in the new Residence, as exemplified by the works from the studio of Tuthmosis and his colleagues. This was the period of the head of Nefertiti now in Berlin, and of the lifelike gypsum masks, which appear to be genuine portraits.

6

The Pure Teaching

New Sanctuaries for the Aten

In the new Residence, the Aten's followers found themselves in an ideal setting for their endeavors, one where they could devote themselves undisturbed to the service of the new teaching, which now attained its perfection.

Temples and tombs were not rendered superfluous by Akhenaten's teaching, despite the many innovations it entailed. The sanctuaries of the Aten constituted the spiritual center of the new Residence of Akhetaten, while on his boundary stelae the king made specific provisions for the preparation of tombs in the eastern mountain. But the structure and meaning of these constructions differed fundamentally from those of the past.

Previously, every Egyptian temple had been understood as a shrine for the cult image of a deity. Since the Aten had no image aside from the radiant sun, the whole world was in fact his shrine. And since his cult image was accessible only to prayers and offerings, all the richness of the daily cult ritual that had been celebrated in each of the innumerable temples, with its purification, anointing, and clothing of the divine image, no longer applied. This was not without consequences for the forms assumed by the new cultic structures.

Along with the introduction of the new artistic style, we

discern in the representations a new type of architecture: the Aten temple. Like all Egyptian sanctuaries, it was sheltered from the outside world by high walls (this was true, at least, of the temple at Amarna), but it was open above to the sunlight, which had previously had only limited access to the columned halls and chambers. Even the doorways now had broken lintels, while the processional way through the middle of the columned halls was unroofed. To diminish the play of shadows, doorways were provided with raised thresholds.

Thus, wherever he strode, the king was in contact with his god. As shown in the representations, every cultic act actually did take place under the radiant sun. And because there was sunlight everywhere, even in the interiors of the buildings, it was practical to employ only sunk relief, which heretofore had been reserved for exterior walls.

A further consequence of the new beliefs was that there was no longer a need for a holy of holies, a sanctuary for an earthly cult image of the god fashioned out of costly materials. As soon as the Aten rose in the morning, he filled the temple completely with his presence, as stressed in the text of the earlier boundary stelae: "by means of his rays, he fills it with himself." The temple thus now had no real axis, and the king's processional way ended at an elevated altar dedicated to the cult of the sun.

The Aten's effect on his temple and the world was not worked through words he spoke to Pharaoh, but through his rays. His life-maintaining and life-giving hands were present everywhere in the sanctuary. And so that they might take hold of offerings everywhere they touched, the sanctuary was now overfilled with altars on which food lay ready for the god. Among these (we must not deceive ourselves) there were still sacrificial offerings, cattle and geese, and the Aten temple had its own slaughterhouse. But all these were decked with flowers, which were now the preferred offering. And the offering was still always accompanied by the singing of hymns and by music and incense.

However much the king stressed that he lived on Maat, he was now obliged to abstain from representing Maat as a goddess and, with that, from the heretofore popular scene, laden with symbolism, of the presentation of Maat. Its replacement was probably the proffering of votive figures that tended to be decorated with feathers, producing again a reference to Maat, for her name could also be written with the hieroglyph of a feather. The figures tended to be connected with cartouches, and this practice would later be continued in the Ramesside Period, when the king offered his throne name, compounded with the concept of Maat, to a deity. As so often, Nefertiti took an active part in these cult scenes—in no other period was a queen so intensively involved in the divine cult as at Amarna. She was a member of the triad that the royal couple formed along with Aten, and which replaced the triads of Thebes (Amun–Mut–Khons) and Memphis (Ptah–Sakhmet–Nefertem), which had previously stood at the head of the pantheon.

A Holy Family

Family scenes, in which all six daughters now often appear, also displaced earlier scenes of deities and their mythological constellations. Intimately and emphatically, the royal family display the love that reigns among its members—a love that, because it is pleasing to the Aten, is supposed to emanate over all the world. The daughters caress one another or are affectionately tended to by their parents. They sit on their parents' laps, and once, on a fragment in the Louvre, Nefertiti appears on Akhenaten's lap (Figure 17). In any other period, it would have been unthinkable to represent Pharaoh eating and drinking, as happens in the tombs at Amarna.

As far as its ground plan and its conception are concerned, the temple remained a processional route with a stress on its central axis—though no longer a route for a deity whose image would leave the temple, but rather one for the king who entered it. The royal family's departure by chariot replaced the divine barque processions on festival days.

FIGURE 17. *The royal family on Akhenaten's lap. After N. de G. Davies,* The Metropolitan Museum of Art, the Egyptian Expedition *1922/23, p. 42, fig. 4.*

Like its predecessors, the processional temple was made up of pylons, courtyards, and columned halls. Representations show that the facade of the great Aten temple at Amarna was adorned with ten flagpoles, thus surpassing the temple of Karnak with its eight. Innumerable statues of the royal couple filled the empty spaces between the columns, but it seems that statues of officials were no longer set up in the temple to share in the daily cult and its offerings.

Such a share in the cult was not possible for the officials, for their place was outside the temple. An unusual tomb scene depicts the police chief Mahu kneeling before heaped-up offerings after being rewarded by the king and praying to Aten for the king's health; exceptionally, an official prays here directly to the god, but the scene takes place in front of the closed pylon of the great temple, not inside the sanctuary. For the rest, small places of worship were found in the houses of Akhenaten's followers, where a sort of household altar depicted the royal family under the radiant Aten. Here, they could turn to the holy trinity and venerate Akhenaten as their personal god.

A Change of Name

About four years after the king, the god Aten also received a new royal titulary, one that mirrored the continuing developments in the teaching. There were harbingers of this in new writings of the old name in a strictly phonetic form, avoiding Horus and Re. The divine names Horus and Shu were removed from the new double cartouche, leaving only Aten and Re. The new creed—for this "dogmatic" name is just that!—reads: "Live Re, the ruler of the horizon, who rejoices in the horizon in his name Re the father (?), who returns as Aten" (Figure 18). The god (and the king as well) is otherwise designated as "ruler," an additional stress on the royal rule exercised by light over all the world. In private letters from the new capital, such as those of the "oil-boiler" Ramose to his siblings, the full name of the god was avoided, but even the short form "Aten" was enclosed in a cartouche.

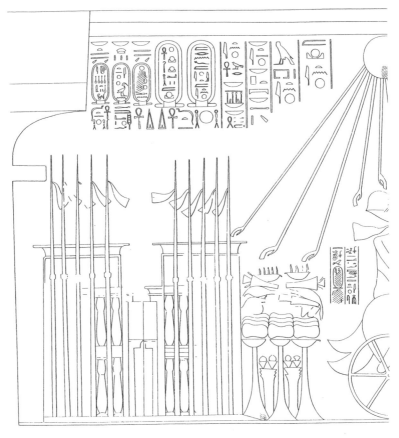

FIGURE 18. *The later form of the didactic name of the Aten, written above the facade of his temple. After N. de G. Davies,* The Rock Tombs of El Amarna, *vol. 4,* Memoirs of the Archaeological Survey of Egypt *16, pl. 20.*

Nothing changed in the representations, and the sole, obligatory icon of the god of light remained the sun disk with its rays and hands. Since he was in the sky, the image of the god is *above* the king in all scenes depicting the cult, not in front of him. And as indicated by the protective uraeus-serpent in the middle of the disk—previously it had appeared on its side—the sun in the sky and thus also the god is to be understood as viewed frontally. From the Egyptian point of view, a frontal view meant the greatest possible effectiveness, which was hoped for here from the god of light. There could be no statues of this god—"sculptors do not know him," as it is stated in the earlier text of the boundary stelae—for how could the light that ruled the world be represented in sculpture in the round? A statue in the Brooklyn Museum published by Robert S. Bianchi in 1990, which he wished to connect with Aten (though he argued that it was created under Amenophis III), is no exception. The disk (without a uraeus!) that replaces its head has parallels in relief sculpture, all relating to the sun god, so that we doubtless have here an image of the traditional god. In the New Kingdom, it was possible to replace the head of a deity with an object, thus further intensifying the symbolic possibilities of "mixed forms."

The essence of this god is the special concern of Akhenaten's "Great Hymn to the Aten," which is perhaps to be ascribed to him personally. It was recorded in the rock tomb of Aya, where it survived through the ages until 1890, when a portion of it was maliciously destroyed during a quarrel among local inhabitants, though it is preserved in a copy made earlier by Urbain Bouriant. We thus have the complete text of this poem, in which Akhenaten's ideas found their purest expression.

The Great Hymn to the Aten

The first lines of the text contain the titles and names of Aten, Akhenaten, and Nefertiti. The actual hymn begins with the words "he says" (referring to Akhenaten).

Beautiful, you appear
in the horizon of the sky,
oh living sun,
who determines life!
You have appeared on the eastern horizon
and filled every land with your beauty.
You are beautiful, great and shining,
high over all the land.

Your rays embrace the lands
to the limit of all you have created.
You are Re when you reach their borders
and bow them down to your beloved son.
You are distant, though your rays are on earth;
you are in their face, though your course is inscrutable.

When you set in the western horizon,
the world is in darkness,
in a state of death.
Sleepers are in their rooms,
heads covered, no eye sees the other.
Were all the possessions under their heads robbed,
they would not notice.
Every beast of prey emerges from its den,
and all the serpents bite.
The darkness is a tomb,

the earth lies numb,
its creator has indeed set in his horizon.

In the morning, you rise on the horizon
and are radiant as the sun in the daytime;
you drive off the darkness and cast your rays.
The Two Lands are in festival daily,
the people awaken
and stand on their feet, for you have roused them.
Clean is their body, they have clothed themselves,
and their arms are (raised) in prayer when you appear,
the whole land does its work.

All cattle are satisfied with their fodder,
trees and foliage bloom.
The birds have flown from their nests,
their wings praise your ka.
All the game animals frisk on their hooves,
all that fly and flutter live
when you have risen for them.
Freighters fare downstream
and back upstream,
every road is open through your rising.
The fish in the river leap before your face,
your rays are within the sea.

Oh you who cause semen to develop in women,
who make "liquid" into people,
who keep a son alive in his mother's womb
and quiet him so that his tears dry up—
you nurse in the womb!—
who give breath
to keep all creation alive.
When (the child) emerges from the womb

to breathe on the day of his birth,
you open wide his mouth
and provide for his needs.

The chick in the egg,
which speaks already in the shell—
you give it breath therein to bring it to life.
You have set its due time
to break (the shell) in the egg;
it emerges from the egg
to speak at its due time,
it is already running about on its feet when it
    emerges from it.

How manifold are your works
which are hidden from sight,
you sole god without equal!
You have created the earth as you desired, quite alone,
with people, cattle, and all creatures,
with everything upon earth
that walks about on feet
and all that is on high and flies with its wings.
The foreign lands of Syria and Nubia,
and the land of Egypt—
you set all in their place and care for their needs,
they all have their nourishment, their lifetimes
    are determined.
Tongues differ in speech,
their characters as well;
their skin colors differ, for you distinguish the peoples.

You create the Nile in the netherworld
and bring it up according to your will
to keep humankind alive, for you have created them.

You are lord of them all, who toils for them,
oh lord of all lands, who rises for them,
oh sun of the daytime, great of majesty!
All the distant foreign lands, you yourself keep them alive,
you have placed a Nile in the sky,
that it might descend to them,
with waves beating on the mountains like the sea,
to water their fields with what they need.
How effective are your plans, oh lord of eternity!
The Nile in the sky, which you give to foreign peoples
and all the creatures of the desert that go on legs;
but the true Nile comes from the netherworld to Egypt.

Your rays nurse all the fields—
when you rise, they live and grow for you.
You create the seasons to make all creation develop—
the winter to cool them,
the heat of summer that they might sense you.
You made the sky far in order to ascend to it
and gaze upon what you have created.

You are unique when you have risen
in all your manifestations as the living Aten
who shines and gleams,
distances himself and comes near;
you create millions of forms from yourself alone—
cities, towns, and fields,
roads and river.
All eyes find themselves facing you,
when you are above the land as the sun of the daytime.

When you have gone, there no longer remains your eye,
which you have created for their sake,

so that you do not behold yourself as the sole one
of what you have created—
even then you remain in my heart,
and there is no one else who knows you,
except for your son, Neferkheperure Waenre,
whom you have taught your nature and your might.

The world comes into being from your gesture, as
you have created it.
When you rise, they live,
when you set, they die;
you are lifetime itself, one lives through you.
Eyes rest on beauty until you set,
all work is laid down when you set in the west.
The rising one strengthens all arms for the king,
and speed is in every foot.

Since you founded the world, you rouse them
for your son, who emerged from your body,
the king of the two Egypts, who lives on Maat,
Neferkheperure Waenre,
the son of Re, who lives on Maat,
the lord of diadems, Akhenaten, great in his lifetime,
and the great king's wife, whom he loves,
the mistress of the Two Lands, Neferneferuaten Nefertiti,
who lives and is rejuvenated
for ever and ever.

For the hieroglyphic text, see Norman de Garis Davies, The
Rock Tombs of El Amarna, *vol. 6, Memoirs of the Egypt*
Exploration Society 18 (London, 1908), plates 27 (drawing)
and 41 (photograph).

Comparing the "Great Hymn to the Aten" with traditional solar hymns, it is striking how the plenitude of mythic images that characterizes the latter has been replaced by the pure contemplation of nature. The hymn of Suti and Hor from the reign of Amenophis III anticipates this to some extent, but now there is no longer an interest in the primeval creation of the cosmos—Aten, "who built himself with his own hands," continually creates the world by means of his light, which is pure presence and thus in no need of a mythical past or a distant primeval time. In contrast to earlier hymns, there is also a lack of any comparisons, for this god can be compared with nothing and no one.

Before and after the Amarna Period, Pharaoh was wished the lifetime of Re, the years of Atum, or the jubilees of Tatenen. Now, the wish was for jubilees like "the sand on the shore, the scales of fish, and the hairs of cattle" (in his tomb, Aya also adds "the feathers of birds and the leaves of the trees"), and the king was supposed to remain "here," in his new Residence of Akhetaten, "until the swan turns black and the raven turns white, until the mountains get up and walk, and until water runs upstream." Undesirable associations were eliminated even in designating the boundaries of the king's sovereignty. Previously, his northern boundary had extended "as far as the darkness," but now it reached "as far as the sun (Aten) shines," for darkness would have been too reminiscent of older mythological concepts.

The Universal Deity: Light

As depicted in the "Great Hymn to the Aten," the god's care extends to distant lands beyond Egypt—"each one has his nourishment, his lifetime is determined." This sentiment was a product of the times, for in the "Book of Gates," which might have been composed in the reign of Amenophis III and is first attested under Haremhab, we have the famed representation of the four races of humankind in the afterlife, and there, too, they are all accorded their lifetimes and their provisions. Ramesses II would later take up the theme when, after concluding a treaty with the Hittites, he spoke of the friendship of the two previously inimical great powers; on his "marriage stela" it is said, "They ate and they drank together and were of *one* accord, like brothers, . . . peace reigned among them." Akhenaten's Aten, who shone on *all* humankind, was especially suited to be a universal god whom all lands could worship.

The omnipresence and the effect of light has also inspired some to a belief in the divine in more modern times. In their last conversation on March 11, 1832, Johann Wolfgang von Goethe confided to his assistant Johann Peter Eckermann that he was prepared to "revere the Sun . . . for he is likewise a manifestation of the highest Being, and indeed the most powerful which we, the children of the earth, are allowed to behold. I adore in him the light and the productive power of God; by which we all live, move, and have our being— we, and all the plants and animals with us." And in his *Memories, Dreams, Reflections,* after depicting the rejoicing of African baboons at sunrise, Carl Gustav Jung states, "The *moment* in which it becomes light *is* God. That moment brings redemption, release. To say that the *sun* is God, is to blur and forget the archetypal experience of that moment."

Was Akhenaten planning a universal religion, as Breasted thought? A universal picture of godhead perhaps emerges from the Great Hymn, and at the beginning of his reign, the king in any case had a sanctuary with the name Gempaaten ("the Aten has been found") erected in Nubia, and perhaps one in Syria as well. Thus, at the beginning, he actually did wish to announce the glad tidings that the Aten had been "found" to all the world under Egyptian sovereignty; Jan Assmann has shown that at Amarna, this "discovery" represented the revelation of the god. Alexandre Moret saw in Aten a god of all humankind, who corresponded to Egypt's international empire in the New Kingdom. But the sources from later in the reign in no way point in this direction.

With the construction of Akhetaten, which also had a Gempaaten temple of its own and constituted a "horizon" for the god, the area in which the new religion was valid became a highly restricted one, for all practical purposes circumscribed by the boundary stelae of the new Residence. The king seems to have erected few buildings, such as those at Memphis and Heliopolis, outside this sacred precinct dedicated to the Aten. Not once is it stated that he had the intention of converting all of Egypt to belief in Aten, and less still is there talk of a mission beyond the borders of Egypt. In the documentation from the archive of diplomatic correspondence, faith in the Aten remains a concern of Egypt alone. We also see no indication that the existing temples of the gods were converted into sanctuaries of the Aten; the worship of the god had its unequivocal center in the new capital. At the same time, only fifteen miles away in Neferusi, Khnum, Thoth, and Osiris were still being worshiped! It would certainly be interesting and instructive to know what was happening during Akhenaten's later years in, for example, the sanctuaries at Elephantine, whether a cult was being celebrated there and for whom; but our sources allow no answer to such questions. We must imagine that the suppression of the old cults was not altogether consistent in the distant provinces, and that Thebes surely was a special case.

7

The Question of Monotheism

Persecution of the Old Deities

At the time the god's name was changed, or just a little later, Akhenaten took the final and most radical step in the development of his teaching. Now there would be no gods but Aten, and the physical existence of the old deities would be obliterated by the erasure of their names and sometimes of their representations as well. The persecution that now ensued was directed especially against Amun and his consort Mut, but it sporadically affected a number of other deities as well, and even the writing of the plural noun "gods." It appears that Thoth, the god of the moon, of wisdom, and of the scribal arts was not affected, and the persecution was otherwise not especially consistent. But care was taken to erase the name of Amun even from the letters in the diplomatic archive, commemorative scarabs, and the tips of obelisks and pyramids; the distant regions of Nubia were also affected, as far as Gebel Barkal at the Fourth Cataract of the Nile. In some instances, Akhenaten even had his own original personal name Amenophis mutilated in his effort to do harm to the hated Amun. This ferocity was surely aimed not only at the heretofore predominant state god but at the "refuge of the poor," which Amun had increasingly become—in the Ramesside Period, he would become a special focus of personal piety, thus occupying the very position claimed by Akhenaten.

The persecution also affected theriomorphic symbols of deities, such as the vulture of Mut and the goose of Amun. Only the falcon and the uraeus-serpent were still allowed, and we hear nothing more of the Mnevis bull of the sun god, for which Akhenaten had made provisions in the text of the boundary stelae. It is indicative that all representations of Akhenaten as a sphinx are connected with the earlier name of the Aten; later, this theriomorphic representation of the king was also abandoned.

Egypt had never experienced an iconoclasm of such dimensions, though the erasure of names had rather often served as a political means, for the name was an inseparable component of a personality, in which and by means of which a person could suffer harm. Erasure of a name meant consignment to oblivion, and because depictions embodied reality in Egypt, erasures were entailed in any persecution.

Egypt as the "Cradle of Monotheism"?

The blow struck at the many deities of the traditional pantheon was a clear sign that Akhenaten was now intent on the uncompromising realization of a more or less strict monotheism. To this extent, the characterization of Egypt as the "cradle of monotheism" has its justification. But there has been debate as to whether monotheism already existed in Egypt before Akhenaten. To clarify this question, we must reach back in time a little. And in this connection, it is helpful to speak in terms of a "concept of the 'one'" (as Jan Assmann called it, following Werner Beierwaltes) rather than the problematic concept "monotheism," and to inquire into the role of the "one" in the history of Egyptian religion.

At the beginning of the modern era, there was a naive belief that God had revealed himself as the One to Adam, and thus to the first man, with the result that monotheism existed from the very beginning, and that polytheism appeared only later, as the result of a "break" with God. In the early days of Egyptology, there was a generally held opinion that at the idealized beginning of history, there was worship of a single deity in Egypt as well, a beneficent counterweight to the "jackal-headed" gods of the supposedly abstruse polytheism that represented a later degeneration. Ancient Egypt could thus already count as "rational" in the eyes of the Enlightenment.

Later, however, the discovery and study of the Pyramid Texts, from 1881 on, made it clear that there was a plenitude of divine names and forms in these earliest religious texts, and that a deity whom the Egyptians addressed and revered as the "one" over against the many was nowhere to be found. Gaston Maspero, who discovered these texts, was thus the first to support the idea of an original polytheism in Egypt. But the use of the absolute, singular noun "god" in personal names, in generalizing statements, and in wisdom literature remained a source of confusion. Statements like "(the) god punishes," "(the) god loves," "(the) god gives," and the like, made it seem as though, in these contexts at least, there were Egyptians who subscribed to a monotheism "for the initiated," while on a more superficial level, the people subscribed to an erroneous multiplicity of divine figures. In this, it was overlooked that the plural noun "gods" and actual divine names also occur in the very same sources. There is thus no question of a monotheism in these texts, but rather of generally valid statements that for various reasons were not to be restricted to any particular deity.

Nevertheless, the notion of an original monotheism gained respectability yet again, especially in the monumental work *Der Ursprung der Gottesidee: eine historisch-kritische und positive Studie* [The origin of the idea of God: A historical-critical and positive study], by Father Wilhelm Schmidt, which appeared in twelve volumes from 1926 to 1949 and was supplemented by essays in the journal *Anthropos*. In the field of Egyptology, Hermann Junker adopted Schmidt's ideas and attempted to establish the existence of an anonymous high god (called the "Great One") in the Old Kingdom. But he met with little assent, and it was not until Étienne Drioton attempted in 1948 to demonstrate the existence of monotheism long before Akhenaten's reform in his *Le monothéisme de l'ancienne Égypte* [Monotheism in ancient Egypt] that the hypothesis again became popular. Thus, when Joachim Spiegel wrote in 1953 in his *Werden der altägyptischen Hochkultur* [Development of Egyptian civilization] that "pure monotheism was thus the reigning form of Egyptian religiosity from the beginning of the historical period" (p. 86), he was expressing a notion that had been widespread prior to 1880, and which would once again determine characterizations of Egyptian beliefs regarding the divine until the appearance in 1971 of my book *Der Eine und die Vielen* (English translation: *Conceptions of God in Ancient Egypt: The One and the Many*, 1996), which attempted to investigate the question on a broader basis. Since that time, the hypothesis of an original monotheism has not reappeared; perhaps it now belongs definitively to the "history" of ideas, along with the idea of a "monotheism for the initiated," a *dieu des sages*.

But discussion of Egyptian religious belief is ongoing, and

the concept of an "idea about the 'one'" has opened up new avenues of approach. With the "one," Egyptian thinking concerned itself above all with understanding creation, and in this respect we can speak with a certain justification of an "original monotheism," for the divine was supposed to have been originally one and then differentiated himself only in the process of creation: "the one who became millions," as it is stated in a formulation popular after the time of Akhenaten. The Egyptians were always fascinated by the attempt to understand this derivation of multiplicity from an original unity, and they tended to describe this ultimately incomprehensible process by means of paradoxical statements regarding the unity.

A wealth of such statements is to be found as early as the Coffin Texts of the Middle Kingdom. There, the god Khepri created his own parents ("I engendered my father and was pregnant with my mother"), and Horus was born "when Isis (his mother!) did not yet exist"; similarly, Orion could state regarding the divine role of a deceased person, "He is my son, older than I." In the New Kingdom hymns to the sun god, statements of this sort were applied to Amun, Re, or Ptah: the creator god was "the 'one,' who engendered his engenderers, who bore his mother," or "the one who bears without having been born." Along these lines, there is Akhenaten's address to Aten, "You are the one who created what does not exist."

The solution to this paradox regarding the beginning of creation was that the original divine unity secreted something of his substance, whether as spittle, sweat, tears, semen, or even as the word that went forth from his mouth. The first divine pair, and thus plurality, resulted from this original emanation. As early as the Coffin Texts, this process was described with a "trinitarian" formula: "when he was one, when he became three." Multiplicity and the plurality of divine forms were thus derived from an original unity.

The Cosmic God of the Ramesside Period

After Akhenaten, and clearly as a result of the impression made by his monotheistic attempt, there was further thinking about the "one," as attested above all in hymns of the Ramesside Period. In this thought, the entire cosmos becomes a manifestation and a revelation of the "one," which is now a cosmic god who is sun and moon, sky and netherworld, water and air, who holds space and time in his hands, and who is also a recourse for individuals in need. This god is thus more comprehensive than Akhenaten's Aten, and though he leaves room for all the other gods, he is also paramount over them all while concealing his own essence from them. As a papyrus in Leiden formulates it,

> He is more distant than the sky,
> he is deeper than the netherworld.
> No god knows his true form,
> his image is not unfolded in the writings,
> one teaches nothing certain about him.

The Ramesside theologians saw or suspected the concealment of the "one" behind the visible, polymorphic cosmos, and behind the divine world as well. Is this pantheism, or is it the "monotheism of concealment" which Jan Assmann wishes to distinguish from Akhenaten's "monotheism of revelation"? It seems rather—and this is more suited to Egyptian religious thought—that we have here the continuation of the paradox of the "beginning." This cosmic god is ever still the "one" who existed before creation, though by taking action he transformed himself into the "millions" in which he remains visible to the eye. This "one"—and this distinguishes him from Akhenaten's god and from that of every monotheism—can therefore also be worshiped in the multiplicity of actual divine forms. Taken together, they constitute his body; they cannot be separated from him, and they share in his essence. In the Late Period, this concept was expressed pictorially by representing the cosmic god as a composite form made up of depictions of a great variety of divine beings joined together in a unity—the "one with nine forms," as he is called in a magical text.

The Monotheistic "Cosmic Formula"

Akhenaten "found" (as he formulated it) the Aten by means of intellectual endeavor or intuition—that is, he discovered the world's dependence on light and believed it could be understood as the central principle from which all could be derived, a cosmic formula that embraced everything in itself. But with light, he committed himself to the visible and was constrained to deny everything that did not belong to the visible world: darkness, the afterlife, and the deities of the pantheon, especially Amun, the "Hidden One"!

In the early years of Akhenaten, it was said of the sun god that "there is no other god like him (*mi qedef*)," while in the tombs of the new Residence we read that "there is no other but him (*wepu heref*)." Therein lies the decisive step toward monotheism and its exclusivity. Correspondingly, the king was now "unique like Aten, there being no other great one but him" (from the tomb of Aya), while in the "Great Hymn to the Aten," the king proclaims, "There is no other who knows you"—in biblical language, "You shall have no other gods before me" and "No one comes to the Father but by me"! (Revised Standard Edition)

There has been constant debate as to whether we have to do here with a "true," consistent monotheism, for even the Aten formed a trinity with the royal couple, which relativizes the oneness of the god. Like so many concepts, monotheism cannot be defined with absolute strictness or effectuated in reality. But with its relentless rigor, this religion of light was the simplest and clearest religion that had ever been devised!

The Aten's monotheistic character is displayed on three levels. One is to be seen in formulations such as "no other but him," which lay claim to exclusivity; additionally, he had neither a female partner nor an opponent, so that nothing existed besides him. Here, Akhenaten's thinking is more radical than that of Deutero-Isaiah ("Besides me there is no god," Isaiah 44.6) or that of Islam; in its rigor, it has been surpassed only by tendencies in Islamic mysticism, for which existence itself is incompatible with the existence of God, for there can be nothing besides God.

The second, more tangible level consists of the persecution of the old deities, which clearly signaled that there was to be no god but Aten. Not until Christianity was there a renewed attempt to eliminate the plethora of deities in favor of the One! And the third level is that of the cult, which from the beginning of Akhenaten's reign was directed solely and exclusively to the Aten (also in his names of Re and Re-Harakhty) on all official monuments.

8

Belief in an Afterlife without a Hereafter

Osiris in the Shadow of the New Light

Amun, the state god who was later to suffer so much persecution, still appeared on early monuments of Akhenaten; but
from the very beginning there was a striking abstinence vis-
à-vis Osiris, the ruler of the dead and of the netherworld, the
realm of the afterlife. This points to a profound change in
beliefs regarding the afterlife, one in which there no longer
was room for Osiris. At Amarna, even the title "Osiris" disappeared, which heretofore every deceased person had borne
and would bear again later. This system of thought, which
made light its absolute reference point, had great difficulty
with the dark side of the world. Nighttime negated the Aten
and signified death—"They sleep, as though dead," as it is
formulated in the Great Hymn, and, still more concisely,
"When you rise, they live, and when you set, they die!"

The total dependence of all existence on light, which is the
Aten, was now a given. Previously, the night had also been
filled with life, and traditional solar belief had pictured the
nightly journey of the sun through the netherworld in loving
detail. But now, the nocturnal phase no longer meant the
regeneration of light in the darkness, but merely its absence.
Where the sun tarries so long is never stated; the Aten is

quite simply "gone," though his normal location is "in the sky." The moment of his return is the critical one, which all creation jubilantly greets and which ends his nightly absence.

The wakening of the dead to new life was no longer accomplished nocturnally in the netherworld, but in the morning, in the light of the rising sun and at the same time as those still alive. All was now oriented toward the east, and indeed, even the tombs lay in the eastern mountain of Akhetaten—in the text of the earlier boundary stelae Akhenaten gave directions to prepare his tomb there, "where the sun rises"; the "West," previously the mortuary realm on whose "beautiful ways" the blessed dead had walked, disappeared from the concept of the world. Generally, insofar as hymns to the setting sun were written (an example is furnished by the tomb of the overseer of the harem, Meryre), the talk is not of the sun's stay in the netherworld, but only of Akhetaten.

The Afterlife Becomes This-worldly

Like the form of the mummy, the tombs were now mere shells for the body. The dead did not live in their tombs but on earth. Only very seldom is there mention of the *Duat*, the traditional realm of the dead; thus, Suti expresses a wish to leave the Duat in the morning to gaze upon the sun as it rises daily, "without ceasing." Basically, there was no longer a hereafter, and especially no netherworldly realm of the dead. The world of the dead was not distinct from that of the living, and the Aten of the daytime shone over both.

The boundary between this life and the next was also blurred by the door frames of the dwellings. From as early as the Old Kingdom, it was common to display the titles and name of the owner of a tomb on its entrance, so that he would be visible to all who passed by. Now, such "calling cards" in stone also marked the entrances to living quarters, transferring the afterlife into the this-worldly environment of Akhetaten.

When the Aten rose in the morning, he filled the temple with his light and his presence, received the offerings made by the royal couple, and cared for the needs of both the living and the dead—for the *ba*-souls of the deceased also drew near at that moment to receive their food, which they continued to need, in the form of offerings. In their tomb inscriptions, Huy and other officials describe how their *ba*s are summoned to eat in the temple, where they receive bread, beer, roasted meats, cool water, wine, and milk, while the Aten continues to supply them with the necessary breath of life. This new role of the *ba*-soul, which enters the temple freely, able to receive all sorts of offerings "without being blocked from what it desires," is specific to the Amarna Period but did have some influence thereafter. One such effect was on the popular scene with the tree goddess, where the *ba*, in the form of a bird, would be given food and drink along with the deceased, a charming extension of the motif. In the tomb, one could now do without a false door, which had heretofore been the actual cult place: it was meaningless for the *ba*, with its freedom of movement, and even the corpse had no need of it, for it no longer made the crossing between this world and the next. Pure, corporeal continued existence or regeneration was entirely irrelevant at Amarna; what was crucial was existence as a "living *ba*." Nevertheless, there remained the wish that the *ba* might again unite with the corpse, for only thus could the totality of a person be established.

In his tomb, Tutu makes an express reference to the analogy between life and death: "You stand up in your tomb in the morning to see the Aten when he rises. You wash yourself

and clothe yourself as you did when you were on earth. . . .
You arise and forget weariness"; afterwards, freshly animated
by the rays of the Aten, he would accompany the god "like
the blessed in the hall of the House of the Benben (a temple)." The principal yearning of mortal beings was to gaze
upon the Aten and follow him, and to breathe the "sweet
breath of the north wind (or of life)"; the decisive moment
of existence was awakening in the morning, which signified
the renewal of life.

On the lintel of Hatiay in the Louvre, which probably
stems from the early years of Akhenaten, when the old deities
were still worshiped, the deceased prays before Osiris, Isis,
Sokar, and Hathor, expressing the wish that he might go out
(from the tomb or the netherworld) as a living *ba* "to see the
Aten on earth." In a longer prayer, Osiris is invoked as the
sun; his essence has merged fully with that of the sun god
Re, for "his disk is your disk, his image is your image, his
majesty (*shefyt*) is your majesty." This solution builds on inti-
mations in the Litany of Re, and it would result in a total
amalgamation of the two gods on the coffins of Dynasty 21.

In the Litany of Re, whose ancient Egyptian title was
"Book of Adoring Re in the West," and which originated at
the beginning of the New Kingdom, seventy-five invocations
of the sun god in his nocturnal, netherworldly aspects are
illustrated with figures that serve to depict the epithets and
functions that are invoked. These include depictions of Osiris,
who was becoming ever more widely perceived as the sun at
night and connected with Re as the "united" deity, as he is
called in the title and text of the Litany. In a next step, this
"United One" received the ram's head of the nocturnal sun
god—in a hymn from the Memphite tomb of Haremhab, and
thus shortly after Akhenaten, Osiris is already called "ram-
headed," and, beginning with the tomb of Nefertari, he could

also be represented as such. But despite this close affinity with the sun god, Akhenaten preferred to banish Osiris entirely from his concept of the afterlife; he did not allow him to serve even as the nocturnal manifestation of the sun, for his popularity would easily have made him a competitor to the worship of Aten.

Living On in the Temple

The realm of the dead, as Akhenaten and his intimates saw it, lay in the temple of the Aten at Akhetaten; for this reason Meryre, the overseer of the harem, called himself "justified in Akhetaten," while the general Ramose was styled "possessor of provisions (*imakh*) in Akhetaten." One was no longer obliged to trust in a distant "Field of Reeds" or "Field of Offerings" to feel certain of provisioning after death. All the spells that had previously been needed for orientation, supplies, and protection in the fields of the hereafter became unnecessary—there was no Book of the Dead in the actual Amarna Period, just as the royal books of the netherworld were no longer used. And we now understand why architecture played such a role in the decoration of the tombs of the officials at Amarna—temple and palace were indeed the new realm of the dead, one located in this world!

The question arises, What sort of next-worldly destiny was conceivable outside Akhetaten? In his tomb at Saqqara, the vizier Aper-El was called "justified in the west of Memphis"; he thus counted on a continued existence there, though in this case we are quite likely dealing with the early years of Akhenaten. In the provinces, there are no tombs dating with certainty to his later years. But we can imagine that the *ba*-soul, as a human component endowed with freedom of movement, visited the nearest Aten temple or, even better, the chief temple at Akhetaten in order to participate in the regular offerings and the proximity of the king; Akhenaten was now in fact present only in his Residence. By way of comparison, we may cite the older concept that all human *ba*s would accompany the sun god in his barque, just as they all now made their way to the temple. Thus, in its beliefs regarding the afterlife, the Aten religion embraced no universal outlook, but rather a narrowly bounded regionalism.

External Forms

Although the concept of life after death experienced a radical change, existing funerary customs and forms, such as burial rites and the traditional grave goods, were preserved. But mourning and burial in the form of a mummy are represented in only one official's tomb at Amarna—that of Huy—on the east wall! Since only daytime existence, in the light of the Aten, counted now, a mummy was in fact unnecessary, and regeneration of the body in the afterlife no longer played a role. For this reason, the scarab beetle, the most important symbol of regeneration, disappeared from the output of the royal workshops; in its place, there was the neutral form of the finger ring. Scarabs bearing the name of Akhenaten are thus extremely rare. On the other hand, many royal *shawabti*s in an unmistakable Amarna style are preserved to us—mortuary figurines that served as workers who were supposed to carry out burdensome labor that might be required of the deceased in the afterlife. Traditionally, they were inscribed with a spell from the Book of the Dead, which designated the deceased as an "Osiris"; Akhenaten's figurines bore only the title and name of the king. Of the relatively few private *shawabti*s from this period, some are inscribed in the traditional manner—even in the case of a "chantress of the

Aten"!—while some bear an offering formula containing the name of the Aten.

We must assume that a royal tomb at Thebes had been planned for Akhenaten at the beginning of his reign, though until now it has not been located with certainty. "Magical bricks" on which the king was still designated as "Osiris" were probably intended for this burial place. In the royal tomb at Tell el-Amarna, fragments of several coffins of pink granite were found; they bear prayers by Akhenaten to the radiant Aten instead of the heretofore usual protective gods, the "Sons of Horus" and Anubis. It is significant that the queen stood at all four corners of his sarcophagus: under Tutankhamun, she would be replaced by the protective goddesses Isis, Nephthys, Neith, and Selkis. Nefertiti was thus Akhenaten's protective goddess, who wished him pleasant breath for his mouth and nose. On the other hand, he employed the "neutral" form of the falcon as a protective entity on his canopic shrine, for the traditional vulture was too loaded with associations with the old religion. The smaller Aten temple at Akhetaten was presumably intended for his mortuary cult; like the mortuary temples at Thebes, it lay in the immediate vicinity of a palace and bore the designation *huwet*.

The king's precedent of replacing the protective deities with the queen on his coffin was immediately imitated. The coffin of Taat from Deir el-Medina is an important, although thus far unique, attestation of this; here as well, the protective deities are replaced by members of the deceased's family.

The King's Grace Replaces the Judgment of the Dead

Since the afterlife no longer entailed a realm of the dead, the concepts of a general Judgment of the Dead and a vindication in the afterlife were no longer suited to the times. The ethical basis for a blessed afterlife was now the grace and mercy of the king, who "lived on Maat" and thus embodied, for his officials, the plumb line of her scale of justice. In the next life, as in this one, provisions could be received only from the king. Whoever was loyally devoted to him would survive death as a *Maaty:* one who was an adherent of Maat and thus vindicated. Without this loyalty, there was no life after death, for Akhenaten was the "god of fate (Shai), who grants every lifetime and a burial (after) old age in his favor," as stated by the general Ramose in an inscription from his home at Akhetaten. In their tombs, officials were still always designated as "vindicated" (*maa-kheru*). Immediately after the Amarna Period, pictorial representations of the Judgment of the Dead would receive an important new element in the form of "Swallower-of-the-Dead," a female monster composed of a crocodile, a lion, and a hippopotamus; she embodied the very jaws of Hell that devoured the "enemies."

Beliefs regarding the afterlife at Amarna can thus be summarized quite simply: the dead slept at night, and in the daytime they accompanied the Aten and the royal family to the Great Temple, where all were provisioned. There was thus still life after death, but the king was responsible for it as lord of provisions both in this life and the next; the Aten tended personally only to the continued existence of the king. The temple and the palace, with all their painted architectural detail, ruled the new tomb decoration, for they mirrored the new, thoroughly earthly afterlife of the deceased; the departure of the royal family from the palace and the daily offerings made by the king in the temple were also popular themes. Instead of the usual pillars, columns were now employed in the tombs—Aya had an actual columned hall in his—and in this way, too, the realm of the dead took on architectonic form as something belonging to this world, though this particular usage was a continuation of developments under Amenophis III.

In a somewhat murky formulation in the Great Hymn, we learn that even when the Aten has "gone away" at night and left the world in the sleep of death, he nevertheless remains in the heart of the king. That was his enduring place, and the community, together with his prophet, mitigated the solitude that surrounded him in his daily course across the sky. The afterlife of traditional belief, which the sun now no longer touched and illuminated, lost much of its luster. In the tomb of an artisan whose name Paatenemheb points to the Amarna Period, there is the earliest copy of the "Inyotef Song," which was once dated to the Middle Kingdom because of its fictitious ascription to a king named Inyotef. Its skeptical stance vis-à-vis the afterlife, which characterizes the entire new genre of harpers' songs as well as the new laments over the dead, is a product of Akhenaten's religion of light and the deep shadows it cast.

The Inyotef Song

I have heard the words of Imhotep and Hardedef
whose maxims are cited everywhere.
Where are their places? Their walls have collapsed,
their places do not exist, as though they had
*   never been made.*
No one comes from there to describe their condition
and give tidings of their needs
and calm our hearts
until we, too, arrive where they have gone.

*So let your heart rejoice, so as to forget all that—
it is good for you to follow your heart as long as you live.
Place myrrh on your head,
clothe yourself in finest linen,
anoint yourself with genuine oil of the god's property.
Increase your well-being and let your will not grow slack!
Follow your heart together with your beloved,
do your work on earth and let your heart grieve not,
until that day of mourning comes to you.
But the "Weary of Heart" (Osiris) does not hear their cries,
and their laments save no human heart from
    the netherworld.
Again: Spend a happy day, do not weary of it!
Remember: no one can take his goods with him.
Remember: no one who has passed away returns!*

*The entire text is preserved on Papyrus Harris 500 (= British
Museum 10060) from Dynasty 19.*

9

Dark Years

The Eventful Year 12

With the persecution of the old deities, the new religion reached its acme and at the same time went too far. Thus began a final phase, which Donald B. Redford has characterized as a "sunset."

The last two official monuments of the king stem from his twelfth regnal year, and both have to do with his foreign policy. One is a victory stela, several copies of which were probably set up in Nubia; some fragments of one such copy, later reused at the temple of Buhen, were partially published only in 1976, while another was located at Amada. The topic of their inscription is a military expedition against the Nubian land of Ikaita, which Akhenaten entrusted to his viceroy Tuthmosis. The text follows a long-standing model, according to which the "rebellion" of this land is reported to the king, affording him the pretext for a military intervention. This assumed the scale of a relatively modest punitive expedition, as shown by the list of spoils at the end of the inscription: 145 enemies were captured, and eighty were killed, some of them in battle and some "on the stake," that is, by execution. This is the only expedition attested to date for Akhenaten, and he surely did not lead it himself; he thus evaded the established model according to which every pharaoh led an expedition, often only a symbolic one, at the beginning of his reign so as to fulfill his role as a victorious monarch. In other ways as well, he avoided warlike attributes, such as we still find in the reign of his father Amenophis III, and the representation of the triumphal scene of "smiting the enemies" seems to have been absent from the pylon towers of the temple at Amarna. In the correspondence from the Amarna archive, his loyal vassals constantly implore him in vain to intervene militarily in western Asia; this is the origin of the cliché of the "pacifistic" king who remained inactive abroad while wrapped up in his fantasy world at Akhetaten. But toward the end of his reign, we encounter lively foreign policy activity in connection with the visit of the prince Aziru of Amurru to Akhetaten.

The other monument of year 12 is the "tribute of the foreign lands," which is represented in the tombs of two officials at the new Residence. Previously, the "tribute" (actually, trade goods) of foreign peoples had been depicted in the tombs of viziers; nominally the highest civil officials, they also had oversight of foreign trade. Nothing of the sort is found in the tombs of Akhenaten's viziers, Ramose and Aper-El. This stress on foreign policy was probably important to the king because of increasing difficulties on the domestic front; the intensification of his religious policy doubtless incurred reactions, and along with those, there were family problems as well.

Kiya, the Beloved

The royal family idyll we find so compelling in the "intimate" scenes from Amarna art has for some time had its Achilles' heel—ever since we learned of Kiya, the king's favorite. She was mentioned briefly in the scholarly literature for the first time in 1959 and 1961, and in the meanwhile, we have learned more about her through the work of Yuri Y. Perepelkin, Reiner Hanke, Wolfgang Helck, and Rolf Krauss. Her name is a shortened form, behind which lies a different name, perhaps a foreign one. Kiya might have come from the kingdom of Mitanni, for we know of an "administrator of the woman from Naharin" from a funerary cone of the period, though the woman is not identified by name; Kiya is often called simply "the lady" (*ta shepset*), which has led to the suggestion that there is a recollection of her in the anonymous "lady" of the "Tale of Two Brothers" from the Ramesside Period. Even if she was a Mitannian, she cannot have been identical to the princess Tadukhepa, whom Akhenaten inherited from the harem of his father, though she might have been a distinguished and beautiful Asiatic in her retinue; from the text on the commemorative scarab that Amenophis III had issued on the occasion of his marriage to Gilukhepa, we learn this Mitannian princess was accompanied to Egypt by 317 ladies in waiting.

In any event, Kiya is attested side by side with Nefertiti for several years, though the two women are carefully distinguished by their official titles. In the royal harem, there had always been only one "great royal wife," and in the case of Akhenaten, this was Nefertiti. Kiya, on the other hand, bore the highly unusual official title "great beloved wife of the king," which elevated her above all the other women of the harem, but without assigning her any religious significance such as Nefertiti had.

Kiya is also carefully distinguished from Nefertiti in the representations. She never appears wearing a crown or the royal uraeus-serpent, and her name is not enclosed in a cartouche. Additionally, there is never more than one daughter behind her, in contrast to the usually larger number who appear behind Akhenaten and Nefertiti.

Whether or not we must reckon with a "disappearance" of Nefertiti from the scene, and however that would have to be explained, Kiya stood out for a time as the predominant wife at the royal court. In a representation preserved only in fragmentary form, she appears, along with her own daughter, behind Akhenaten under the radiant Aten, while at the same time, Nefertiti's daughters Merytaten and Ankhesenpaaten are lying on the ground in proskynesis and are thus clearly relegated to second rank.

Akhenaten apparently had another, seventh daughter by Kiya, and it can be imagined that the latter established her own daughter as heir to the throne instead of Merytaten. But it can only be left to speculation whether we must reckon with a formal power struggle between Kiya and Merytaten (who in the end bore the title of a queen) in the later years of Akhenaten. It seems certain only that in many instances the name of Kiya was replaced by that of (Princess, not Queen) Merytaten and that part of the burial equipment in the "ominous" tomb 55 was originally intended for Kiya.

The Dakhamanzu Affair

On the other hand, it is unlikely that Kiya wrote the highly political letter to Suppiluliumas in which a widowed Egyptian queen requested a Hittite prince to be her consort. The Hittite sources speak of an actual queen regnant, a "female king of Egypt," which Kiya certainly was not.

This letter is preserved only in Hittite sources and identifies the Egyptian queen only by her title, "Dakhamanzu," not by name. She wrote to Suppiluliumas that her royal husband had died without leaving a son. This excludes Merytaten, who did not outlive Smenkhkare, leaving only Nefertiti, Akhenaten's widow, or Ankhesenamun, the widow of Tutankhamun, as the potential author of the letter. The request for a Hittite prince initially succeeded, but the murder of Prince Zananza while he was en route to Egypt prevented a diplomatic marriage and an alliance of the two great powers at this early date; this was not to be accomplished until nearly a century later, under Ramesses II. Now, however, the assassination of the prince triggered a retaliatory attack on the part of the Hittites; its unfortunate result was an outbreak of pestilence, to which the great Hittite king Suppiluliumas succumbed, and it has been suspected that this plague was the cause of the early deaths of several other leading figures of the Amarna Period.

A "Sunset" Filled with Mystery

The later years of Akhenaten are filled with puzzles and problems, and none of the proposed reconstructions of this period is entirely workable. The supposed disappearance of Nefertiti, which has now again been called into question; the position of Kiya, Akhenaten's favorite; his "marriages" to his older daughters, which served to elevate their status; the problem of a coregency with a female partner or with his son-in-law Smenkhkare; the alleged brief sole rule of Merytaten after the death of her father; and the authorship of the above-mentioned letter to Suppiluliumas—new reconstructions keep surfacing for these eventful but poorly documented years. The lack of sources has proven favorable to a luxuriant overgrowth of speculation.

To note some highlights from these later years, we can

draw on inscriptions on the vessels found in great abundance at Tell el-Amarna. They give the exact year, and more rarely the month, when they were created and filled with perishable products such as wine, oil, and honey. Their distribution over the individual regnal years is quite uneven and indicates what are clearly high points: year 9–10 (new titulary of the god and further changes?), year 12 (tribute of the foreign lands), and year 14 (arrangements for the succession?). The origin of these deliveries is noted, but not their purpose, so that it remains unclear what occasioned them.

Consumption of large quantities of products usually points to divine festivals, but there can have been no question of these at Amarna. Jan Assmann has pointed to the impoverishment of social and religious life which this discontinuance of festivals entailed. Previously, festivals continually afforded fresh opportunities to approach the divine and beseech care and salvation from all sorts of afflictions. Public rewards—the awarding of gold to meritorious officials—could be no substitute for this, and Akhenaten's expectations in this regard would prove to be of no avail: the worship of the traditional deities would flower again in his immediate vicinity, and even satire of the king and his "holy family" would flourish.

Mockery of the "Heretic King"?

The two dozen limestone figurines of monkeys found at Akhetaten might point in this direction. Scenes of chariotry and kissing recall popular motifs in the representations of the royal family; in the Ramesside Period the satiric, theriomorphic distancing of Pharaoh would become quite familiar. Akhenaten's officials might thus have found an outlet, in these groups of monkeys, for expressing their inner distance from the "heretic king."

The discovery of figurines of traditional deities in the houses at Amarna is significant. They must stem from a time when these deities were officially persecuted, thus testifying to their continuing, albeit secret, worship; at the same time, they touch on the area of magic, which was totally excluded from official religion in the Amarna Period. Predominant are figurines of the popular tutelary deities Bes and Taweret, while other deities are attested less often or in only one instance: Sobek, Isis, Thoth, Ptah, Mut, and even the hated Amun, as well as Osiris. Along with the amulets (including the especially popular *udjat*-eye), representations of Bes, Taweret, and Amun were also present in the houses; by way of texts, "laments" are attested, in particular a graffito left behind in a relatively obscure spot in Theban Tomb 139 by Pawah, the "scribe of the divine offerings of Amun" in the mortuary temple of Smenkhkare. In it, he praises his god Amun in terms that in part are reminiscent of the poems of the "Dialogue of a Man Weary of Life with His Soul" and their praise of death—the works of the "critical literature" of the Middle Kingdom were now being circulated anew and are mostly attested to us only in copies of the late New Kingdom, such as our only copy of the "Admonitions of Ipuwer" with its impressive depiction of widespread change and even revolution. After this period of suppression, laments were now transformed into praises of the god who had triumphantly survived all his persecution:

> You give satisfaction without eating,
> you give drunkenness without drinking, . . .
> oh Amun, champion of the poor!
> You are father to the motherless,
> husband to the widow.
> How lovely it is to speak your name,

it is like the taste of life,
it is like the taste of bread for a child,
like a garment for the naked,
like the scent of a flowering twig at
the time of summer's heat.

Turn to us, oh lord of eternity!
You were here when nothing had yet come into being,
and you will be here when it is at an end.
You make me see the darkness that you give—
give me light, that I may see you!

The End Is Uncertain

From the fact that Smenkhkare had a mortuary temple with an Amun cult at Thebes, and that Amun was once again mentioned next to the Aten in two late tomb chapels at Tell el-Amarna, it has been concluded that Akhenaten relented and partially mitigated his reform while he was still alive. Since his coregency with Smenkhkare is once again the subject of debate, this supposition now rests on a shaky foundation. It is possible that Aten's renewed coexistence with the traditional deities began only after the death of Akhenaten and ended some years later when Tutankhaten changed his name.

In any case, there is no indication of a fall from power or a violent end to the "heretic king," so his accomplishments did not come to a halt immediately upon his death. During a transition period that lasted for some years, there was a cautious attempt to carry on his work; it was only then that the pressure of opposing forces proved too strong, leading to the abandoning of Aten and his sacred precinct of Akhetaten. But what was given up immediately after the death of Akhenaten was the sole worship of the Aten (along with the ban on the remainder of the pantheon) and the denial of an afterlife in the netherworld. Everything else could wait, and what was decisive was probably a feeling of relief from a heavy burden, a breath of fresh air after the death of the "heretic king."

10

The Successors

Many Women, but No Heir

The "long lifetime" that Akhenaten regularly bore as an epithet was not granted him; the king died in the prime of life, probably in July 1336 B.C.E. Above all, he died without leaving behind a son who could fill his political and religious role. Nefertiti and Kiya had borne him only daughters; of his siblings, only a sister, Baketamun (later Baketaten) had lived to see his coronation; and Nefertiti seems also to have had only one sister. There was thus a large selection of royal women, but no unequivocal male heir to the throne.

The succession problem was especially tricky on this occasion, because not just a new pharaoh was needed, but rather a son of the god, a mediator between Aten and humankind, a prophet to preserve and to promulgate the pure teaching of the god of light. It is difficult to imagine how the "crown princess" Merytaten, for instance, could have played such a role, one that even the king's two young relatives, Smenkhkare and Tutankhaten (still a child), were obliged to grow into. The "king makers" elevated each of these two young men in turn to the throne, demonstrating in the process that they were seeking no radical break with the ruling dynasty.

In the case of Smenkhkare, it remains unclear whether he

had already been appointed coregent by Akhenaten or whether his rule of about three years began only after the death of the "heretic king." A few monuments heretofore cited in favor of a coregency can be interpreted otherwise. On the stela Berlin 17813, for instance, two kings appear together in full regalia, but they have only three cartouches, as the royal couple Akhenaten and Nefertiti do, so that the "coregent" (wearing the Double Crown!) might rather be the "great royal wife"; on another stela in Berlin (20716), she wears the Blue Crown and is handing Akhenaten a cup of wine. Thus, there is only a single official representation depicting Smenkhkare, with Merytaten as his wife, rewarding Meryre in his tomb. It is possible that the official inserted them immediately after Akhenaten's death, when the abandonment of Akhetaten and its tombs had not yet been decided on, so that even this representation does not afford proof of a coregency. A very fragmentary stela in University College, London, does indeed display four cartouches, thus indicating a coregency, but even here the identity of Akhenaten's partner is debatable. The epithet "beloved of Neferkheprure" or "beloved of Waenre" (both names refer to Akhenaten) is no more than circumstantial evidence that one might choose to connect with a still living "heretic king," and thus with a coregency as opposed to a posthumous worship of Akhenaten.

Tutankhaten Makes His Appearance

We are not on firm ground until the reign of Tutankhaten, though his origin remains uncertain. His designation "beloved king's son" on a block from Hermopolis has often been taken as a justification for viewing him as the son of Amenophis III or Akhenaten, but this Egyptian princely title is too vague to allow any conclusions. Several years ago, near the Red

Monastery at Sohag, the tomb of a "god's father," Senned-jem, to whom the upbringing of the young Tutankhaten was evidently entrusted, was discovered; are we to conclude from this that the prince spent his early childhood in the region of Akhmim, the home of that prominent family from which Teye, Yuya, and Aya stemmed?

On the back of his throne, the new royal couple is represented beneath the radiant Aten, thus continuing the idea of a divine triad which had been realized by Akhenaten, Nefertiti, and the Aten. But this attempt to maintain basic elements of Akhenaten's religion lasted only a short time, for a direct continuation of his reform proved impossible. A first sign of this was the abandonment of the icon of the sun disk with its rays.

Return to Amun and Ptah

The new king's name was evidently changed to Tutankh*amun* in his third regnal year, and immediately thereafter, Akhenaten's "Horizon of Aten" was abandoned. The court was moved to Memphis, whence the text of the "Reformation Stela" proclaimed the end of the reform and the renewal of the old cults that had been "forgotten" for so long that gods and goddesses no longer drew nigh when called upon. At the very beginning of the inscription, the young king is designated as "beloved" of Amun-Re, Atum of Heliopolis, Re-Harakhty, Ptah, and Thoth—an unusual assemblage intended to do justice to all the important cults. There was a prevailing sense that the land had undergone an illness and was finally healed. But there was also the matter of restoring Maat in the wake of that very king who had constantly maintained that he lived on Maat.

The course of religious developments immediately after

Akhenaten can perhaps best be seen in hymns employed by
Haremhab during the reign of Tutankhamun, in particular on
his stela 551 in the British Museum. There, the regent prays
to Atum-Harakhty, commencing with turns of expression
that could have come directly from a hymn to the Aten:

You have appeared on the horizon of the sky
perfect and youthful as Aten . . .

Here, "Aten" is written with a divine determinative, as
though Akhenaten's teaching were still in force, though the
sentence continues with "in the embrace of your mother
Hathor," thus returning, with this mythic reference, to the
traditional embedding of the sun god in "constellations" of
deities. Akhenaten's Aten had no mother, while Haremhab's
hymn mentions both Hathor and the sky goddess Nut as the
mother of the god. A few verses later, the god is extolled as
"king of sky and earth"—which the Aten had also been!—but
also as "ruler of the netherworld (*Duat*) and chief of the
desert, the realm of the dead," and thus once again as lord of
the hereafter, and as the "one who raised himself from the
primeval water (*Nun*)." Following this, cultic reality and the
mythology of the course of the sun once again make their
appearance:

August god in his chapel,
Lord of time in his barque!
Those in the horizon row you . . .
The bas *of the west rejoice at you . . .*

The conclusion is rich in mythological allusions, all in
the style of traditional hymns: "Perfect youth whom Ptah
created, . . . who emerged as Horus . . . ruler of time and

sovereign of the gods of eternity, . . . your mother Nut lifts you up."

There is appended a praise of Thoth, the god of wisdom and the moon, with whom Haremhab directly compares himself—like the moon by the sun, he stands at the side of his king, Tutankhamun. There is also praise of the goddess Maat, who grants him the breath of life. The conclusion contains the traditional mortuary wish to enter and leave the "Field of Reeds"—the Egyptian paradise in the hereafter—and to be in the following of Sokar, the Memphite god of the dead. The hereafter banned under Akhenaten has thus made a complete comeback!

At about the same time, the high priest Parennefer presided over the renewal of the cult of Amun at Karnak; a procession bearing the vase sacred to the god, whose origin lay in the traditional cult, played an important role in this. His tomb at Thebes was discovered not many years ago by Friederike Kampp and Karl-Joachim Seyfried; its model is clearly the royal tomb at Amarna and the tombs of the officials there. There is no longer a radiant Aten, but the scene of sun worship, with its rejoicing on the part of all creation, is drawn from the imagistic realm of Akhenaten's tomb. Its indulgence in the representation of chariots is also derived from Amarna.

The spirit of the times is manifest in the solution found for the decoration of Tutankhamun's tomb upon his premature death. It in no way represents a return to tradition, to the time before Akhenaten; rather, referential derivations from tradition were combined with radical innovations worthy of the Amarna Period and in part taken from the decoration of private tombs. This is also true of the tomb of his successor Aya, which was decorated only four years later. On the walls of both tombs are excerpts from the "Amduat," an old Book of the Netherworld, as well as extracts from the Book of the Dead in the tomb of Aya. Along with the Amduat and the Book of the Dead, the gilded shrines of Tutankhamun offer new compositions, among them the "Book of the Heavenly Cow."

The End of the Dynasty: Aya and Haremhab

In the inscription on the stela of his rock-cut tomb in the vicinity of Akhmim, Aya settles the score with "evil" and the "destruction of Right," and he provides that each person can again make offerings to "his own god," and that "all the deities" will be satisfied that their sanctuaries have been restored. The emphasis is thus quite similar to that of Tutankhamun, and his successor Haremhab also makes an emphatic reference to destruction—he provided for the divine temples, which had become "ruin heaps," and he restored the world to its ideal condition:

> He organized this land and gave it instructions that corresponded to (those of) the time of Re. He renewed the temples of the gods from the delta marshes to Nubia. He fashioned all their images, distinct from what had been earlier, with greater perfection. . . . He distinguished their temples, he created their statues in their correct form from all sorts of precious stones. He searched out all the holy, divine precincts that were ruin heaps in this land, and he founded them anew, as they had been at the beginning of primeval time. He dedicated divine offerings to them as regular daily offerings, along with all sorts of vessels for their temples, cast in gold and silver. He equipped them with *wab*-priests and lector priests from the elite of the army. He assigned them fields and cattle.

Haremhab was closely connected by marriage (to a sister of Nefertiti?) to the royal house of Dynasty 18, but he intentionally made himself out to be the first legitimate ruler since

Amenophis III, who served as his principal model. During his reign, lively building activity commenced anew in the temple of Amun at Karnak, and a great number of *talatat*-blocks from Akhenaten's constructions were reused in his own buildings. Egypt also launched a new and active foreign policy that led to the regaining of lost territories in Syria. The Ramesside Period that followed was taking shape.

11

Epilogue

Failure and Continuity

What was left? Akhenaten had founded no congregation; he had no disciples or apostles to carry on his work after his death. There was only his small circle of followers, who were now bereft of a reference point. Akhenaten had concentrated his teaching so exclusively upon himself as the only one who knew the Aten that it was doomed to perish along with him—in any case, in the extreme form in which he had promulgated it.

And yet, he had set in motion changes that would endure after his passing and exercise influence in several areas. After a brief setback, Late Egyptian survived as the new written language, in which a rich literature soon unfolded, reaching previously unknown heights with its harpers' songs and love lyrics. In art, the zest for motion and the depiction of emotion initiated by Akhenaten remained in force for decades, and the visual joy of Amarna art rippled in ever widening circles through the centuries that followed.

In the area of religion, Amun did not entirely recover his paramount status, and his city of Thebes would never again be the capital. But monotheism had to wait half a millennium and longer to receive a fresh chance in Judaism. In this connection, there has been debate as to whether Akhenaten's monotheistic ideas had an influence on Palestine, as was assumed by Sigmund Freud in particular. The temporal interval is too great to infer a direct influence from the Amarna Period on the monotheism of the Hebrew Bible. But undercurrents that remain hidden to us might certainly have exercised an influence; perhaps the author of Psalm 104 indeed drew upon the Great Hymn to the Aten.

More Than an Episode

Akhenaten and the religion he founded were not just transitory phenomena, as they are so often made out to be. The challenge he posed compelled succeeding generations to rethink questions that had seemed resolved, just as art received new impulses from this debate. As Jan Assmann has put it, "The effect of Amarna religion was to clarify, not to reform. The traditional religion became only ever more self-conscious as a result of this confrontation with its antithesis."

This is especially evident in the case of beliefs about the afterlife. The denial of a hereafter and the realm of Osiris compelled a rethinking of the meaning of the dark half of the cosmos. Light remained dependent on darkness, and the positive value of the latter was never felt as clearly as it was after Akhenaten. There can be no greater contrast to his religion of light than this statement in a solar hymn of Tjanefer, a high priest of Amun in early Dynasty 20, regarding the sun god when he descends to the realm of the dead: "When you come to them . . . you are smoky and dark, for your abomination is light"!

On the one hand, the dependence of all life on light, Akhenaten's positive view of light as salvation; on the other hand, light as an "abomination"—the two are exact polar opposites. For renewal and rejuvenation, light and all life require darkness: it was the *entire* course of the sun, including its nocturnal, netherworldly portion, which replenished the energy of the sun. It is only logical that in the immediate wake of Akhenaten, there was a veritable outpouring of symbolic representations of the daily course of the sun. One of the earliest occurs in the "Enigmatic Book of the Netherworld" on one of Tutankhamun's gilded shrines, which until now has remained without parallels; its dependence on Amarna is visible in the streams of light which link the individual figures in the netherworld to one another and enter into the bodies of the deceased.

The Sun Endures

The scenes of the course of the sun demonstrate, moreover, how much importance was ascribed to the sun, even after Akhenaten's failure. Traditional beliefs about the sun experienced no setback, despite the astonishingly massive reaction to Akhenaten's provocation. But now, greater attention was devoted to the combination of Re *and* Osiris (Figure 19). And in contrast to the reformer's attempt to draw the sun god entirely into *this* world and fill it entirely with his presence, denying all that was next-worldly, the Book of the Heavenly Cow (first attested under Tutankhamun) makes the mythic statement that because of the rebellion of humankind, the sun god withdrew for all time from this world to the sky, while at the same time, he established the netherworld for the dead. Here, there is once again stress on the *distance* and the otherworldly aspect of the divine.

The other clear return was in the royal ideology. After Akhenaten, there were only a few tentative attempts at the worship of Pharaoh as a personal god. An example is Huy, Tutankhamun's Nubian viceroy, who entreated his king to

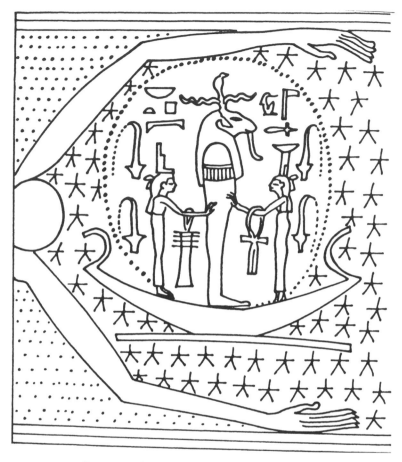

FIGURE 19. *Representation of the course of the sun, with the "combined" form of Re and Osiris. Drawing prepared by A. Brodbeck after a Dynasty 21 papyrus published by A. Piankoff,* Egyptian Religion *4 (1936): 67, fig. 5.*

dispel the "darkness" that meant distance from him. It was Amun who now became the god of the poor and the oppressed, the refuge of the simple in their prayers—the reaction in favor of Amun was thus sustained less by his priesthood than by ordinary folk. As sun god, Amun was both distant and near: distant as a beholder but near as a hearer who stood by those who prayed to him. In the official theology of the Ramesside Period, which was a continuation of the "New Solar Theology," he became a god who filled the entire world with himself (as Aten had filled his sanctuary), the "one" who had made himself "into millions," but without displacing the other deities.

The figure of Shed, the "Savior," the powerful and youthful god who intervened and helped in time of need was another heir to the Amarna Period. Here, in a time of crisis and anxiety, human yearning intensified into a new deity, who was able to step forth, along with Amun, as a personification of help for the needy in this age of personal piety. Basically, he was the young, militant Horus who stood by his father Osiris, but this function was blended with that of the sun god triumphant over his enemies.

The Egyptians evidently accepted the god of light about whom Akhenaten preached in his own creative development of the "New Solar Theology" of Dynasty 18, and they continued to tolerate him for a brief time after the king's reign. "Aten" was never outlawed as a designation of the sun, but what was immediately withdrawn was the exclusiveness with which this new god had made his appearance.

Roots of Fundamentalism

Here, we come to the critical point. In Amarna religion, for the first time in history, an attempt was made to explain the entire natural and human world on the basis of a *single* principle. Like Einstein, Akhenaten made light the absolute reference point, and it is astonishing how clearly and consistently he pursued this concept in the fourteenth century B.C.E., making him in fact the first *modern* human being.

Indeed, modernity also strives to describe the universe with a single formula, to explain it on the basis of a *single* principle; the attempts to do so do not cease.

But Akhenaten demonstrated with unusual clarity that such one-sidedness is doomed to failure; all we repress and ignore will overtake and overshadow us. Akhenaten was perhaps the first fundamentalist in history, and for this reason, he remains even today a very contemporary figure who can scarcely be denied respect and sympathy in any critique of him.

But there is a lesson for us in his fate and his failure: fundamentalism, in whatever form, solves no problems but only suppresses them. We must not succumb to the temptation that from time to time emerges from it and its apparently simple and clear solutions. With its intolerance, it can have no future: things must not be reduced to a single, isolated principle, be it ever so noble and elevated. Always and above all, the whole is at stake.

No grim reaction followed Akhenaten, but rather a cautious attempt to join old to new so as not to give up straightaway what had been achieved on the positive side. The Amarna Period exercised a stimulating and fertilizing influence on the intellectual and spiritual history of ancient Egypt and of all humankind, and, for our own time, it continues to offer a model instance from which we can learn.

Afterword

THIS BOOK has its origins in an Eranos lecture, "Akhenaten—The Rediscovery of a Religion and Its Founder," which was given in Ascona, Switzerland, on August 25, 1988. This was under somewhat dramatic circumstances, for on the previous evening the sole person representing the Eranos Foundation had quite unexpectedly announced that the Eranos Conferences, held annually since 1933, would henceforth be discontinued. In the future, the Eranos Foundation would devote itself only to the *I Ching*, the Chinese book of divination. The lecture on Akhenaten thus marked not only the conclusion of the annual conference on the theme "Concordance or Coincidence," but also the end of the Eranos undertaking altogether, which had been so rich in tradition.

Thereupon, at the last minute, I revised the conclusion of my presentation to stress its relevance. The parallels between Akhenaten's exclusivity and that of the representative of the foundation were just too striking—on the one hand, only the Aten, on the other, only the *I Ching!* I cite the conclusion I revised at that time:

> The fundamentalism rearing its head everywhere today has no future. For Akhenaten has taught us, as has history, which is the most infallible of all oracles, that to be human is to be holistic, and that bigotry leads to nothingness and to ineluctable failure.

For fifty-five years, Eranos has represented the concept of unity in human diversity, and it shall continue to do so wherever this unity is recognized and brought to fruition.

Eranos has been revived. With the help of Tilo Schabert, it has proved possible to form a new association, the Friends of Eranos, and to resume the annual conferences in 1990 with only a single year's interruption. They continue to be held on the tradition-laden Monte Verità at Ascona, annually bringing together a circle of scholars committed to the ideal of a *table ronde*, of discussion that transcends the boundaries of specific disciplines. Each year sees a different constellation of specialties and specialists contributing to a given theme. It is an academy founded on the Renaissance ideal.

Further impetus to expand the original paper came from a symposium on Akhenaten in New York City on December 1, 1990, sponsored by the American Research Center in Egypt; from a series of lectures given at Basel University in the summer of 1994; and from an ever stimulating exchange with Jan Assmann. The completed volume is dedicated to Elisabeth Staehelin in gratitude for many years of productive collaboration.

Bibliography

GENERAL

A bibliography containing more than two thousand titles has been published by G. T. Martin, *A Bibliography of the Amarna Period and Its Aftermath* (London and New York, 1991). A brief overview is provided by H. A. Schlögl, *Echnaton—Tutankhamun: Daten, Fakten, Literatur*, 4th ed. (Wiesbaden, 1993).

The fundamental text collection remains that of M. Sandman, *Texts from the Time of Akhenaten*, Bibliotheca Aegyptiaca 8 (Brussels, 1938). A prosopography has been published by R. Hari, *Répertoire onomastique amarnien*, Aegyptiaca Helvetica 4 (Geneva, 1976).

A selection of relatively recent biographies of Akhenaten: C. Aldred, *Akhenaten, King of Egypt*, 2d ed. (London, 1988); Y. Y. Perepelkin, *The Revolution of Amenophis IV*, 2 vols. (Moscow, 1967 and 1984) (in Russian); D. B. Redford, *Akhenaten, the Heretic King* (Princeton, 1984); H. A. Schlögl, *Amenophis IV. Echnaton*, rororo Bildmonographie, 2d ed. (Reinbek, 1992); F. Cimmino, *Akhenaton e Nefertiti* (Milan, 1987). A review comparing the biographies by Aldred and Redford was published by M. Eaton-Krauss, *Bibliotheca Orientalis* 42 (1990): 541–559, under the title "Akhenaten versus Akhenaten."

CHAPTER I

I presented the initial version of this chapter at a symposium, "Akhenaten: Hero or Heretic?" in New York City on December 1, 1990; see "The Rediscovery of Akhenaten and His Place in Religion," *Journal of the American Research Center in Egypt* 29 (1992): 43–49.

Champollion discussed Amarna in his sixth letter, which he wrote from Beni Hasan and Manfalut; see his *Lettres écrites d'Égypte et de*

Nubie en 1828 et 1829 (Paris, 1833), and the citations in his *Notices descriptives*, vol. 2, p. 320. E. F. Jomard treated the ruins in the *Description de l'Égypte*,vol. 4, pp. 285–436. On the copies by Sicard, see B. van de Walle, *Revue d'Égyptologie* 28 (1976): 12–24; the site had already been called "Psinaula" by the French expedition. Wilkinson published the copies he made in *Manners and Customs of the Ancient Egyptians* (London, 1837), which had many subsequent editions.

C. R. Lepsius published his insights in the *Abhandlungen der Königlichen Akademie der Wissenschaften zu Berlin*, Jahrgang 1851, pp. 157–214; in the text, the page numbers are those of the original volume and the monograph reprint. On Lepsius and Amarna, see also M. Mode, *Das Altertum* 30 (1984): 93–102. Also in doubt as to whether Akhenaten was a woman were Nestor L'Hôte, *Sur le Nil avec Champollion: Lettres, journaux et dessins inédits de Nestor L'Hôte, premier voyage en Égypte, 1828–1830* (Paris, 1840), pp. 66–67, and E. Lefébure, *Proceedings of the Society of Biblical Archaeology* 13 (1891): 479–482 (citing Manetho and the representations of the king).

The most important works on Akhenaten in modern scholarship have already been cited in the chapter. C. C. J. Bunsen's work was translated into English by C. H. Cottrell under the title *Egypt's Place in Universal History: An Historical Investigation* (London, 1948–67). M. Duncker's history was translated by E. Abbott with the title *The History of Antiquity*, 6 vols. (London, 1877–82). The German edition of H. Brugsch's history was translated by H. D. Seymour and P. Smith as *A History of Egypt under the Pharaohs, Derived Entirely from the Monuments*, 2 vols. (London, 1879). G. Maspero's *Histoire ancienne des peuples de l'Orient* (Paris, 1875) had its sixth edition in 1904. Meyer's criticism of Ranke is to be found in *Geschichte des Altertums* (Berlin, 1884), § 146. On Thomas Mann and Egypt, by way of background to his novel *Joseph and His Brothers*, see A. Grimm, *Joseph und Echnaton* (Mainz, 1992), and the contributions in *Thomas Mann—Jahrbuch* 6, 1993 (Frankfurt am Main, 1994).

For J. H. Breasted's characterization, see *A History of Ancient Egypt*, 2d ed. (NY, 1909), pp. 330–331, and *The Dawn of Conscience* (NY, 1933), chap. 15. L. A. White expressed himself critically regarding the stress on Akhenaten's personality in *Journal of the American Oriental Society* 68

(1948): 91–114; for him, Akhenaten was a scholarly fiction created especially by Breasted and Weigall, and the characterization of his god is
decidedly Protestant, not Catholic or Jewish.

On the German and English excavations at Tell el-Amarna, see
Chapter 5. R. Anthes's evaluation is to be found at the beginning of
his monograph *Die Maat des Echnaton von Amarna*, supplement to the
Journal of the American Oriental Society 14 (Baltimore, 1952).

K. Lange, *König Echnaton und die Amarna-Zeit: Die Geschichte eines
Gottkünders* (Munich, 1951). For the citation from Otto, see *Ägypten:
Der Weg des Pharaonenreiches* (Stuttgart, 1953, and numerous later editions), pp. 161–162, 164. J. Spiegel, *Soziale und weltanschauliche Reform-
bewegungen im alten Ägypten* (Heidelberg, 1950), pp. 60–62. For the
citation from K. Jaspers, see *Vom Ursprung und Ziel der Geschichte* (1949),
pp. 68, 74, 77. Van der Leeuw's book bears the title *Achnaton: Een
religieuze en aesthetische revolutie in de veertiende eeuw voor Christus*
(Amsterdam, 1927). See further S. Morenz, *Gott und Mensch im alten
Ägypten*, 2d ed. (Leipzig, 1984), p. 155 (also regarding depictions of
the king in the houses of his officials), and J. Assmann, *The Search
for God in Ancient Egypt* (Ithaca, 2001), p. 199.

CHAPTER 2

Amenophis III and his reign were documented in an exhibit on display in 1992–93 in Cleveland, Fort Worth, and Paris; see the catalogue
by A. P. Kozloff and B. M. Bryan, *Egypt's Dazzling Sun: Amenhotep
III and His World* (Cleveland, 1992), wherein the religious trends of
the period are discussed somewhat too briefly; see also L. Kákosy,
"Die weltanschauliche Krise des Neuen Reiches," *Zeitschrift für ägyptische Sprache und Altertumskunde* 100 (1973): 35–41. On the arts, see
M. Müller, *Die Kunst Amenophis' III. und Echnatons* (Basel, 1988). On
foreign policy vis-à-vis western Asia, which is not treated here, see
especially W. J. Murnane, *The Road to Kadesh*, 2d ed. (Chicago, 1990).
A new translation of the archive of cuneiform correspondence has
been published by W. L. Moran, *The Amarna Letters* (Baltimore and
London, 1992).

On the "New Solar Theology," see J. Assmann, *The Search for God in Ancient Egypt* (Ithaca, 2001), pp. 201–208 (the citation is from p. 208), and idem, *Re und Amun: Die Krise des polytheistischen Weltbilds im Ägypten der 18.-20. Dynastie* (Freiburg and Göttingen, 1983), translated by Anthony Alcock under the title *Egyptian Solar Religion in the New Kingdom: Re, Amun and the Crisis of Polytheism* (London, 1995). On the compositions dealing with the nocturnal regeneration of the sun, see E. Hornung, *Die Unterweltsbücher der Ägypter* (Zurich and Munich, 1992), and idem, *Die Nachtfahrt der Sonne* (Zurich and Munich, 1991).

For the text from the temple of Montu, *see Urkunden des ägyptischen Altertums*, vol. 4 (Berlin, 1984), p. 1668; similarly, from the Third Pylon at Karnak, see ibid., p. 1729.

On the question of Amenophis III's and Akhenaten's "marriages" to their daughters, see Ch. Meyer, *Studien zur altägyptischen Kultur* 11 (1984): 253–263; she wishes to explain the puzzling title as "daughter of the king and the queen." On the crown prince Tuthmosis, see A. Dodson, *Journal of Egyptian Archaeology* 76 (1990): 87–91.

The problem of the coregency is discussed, inter alios, by E. Hornung, *Untersuchungen zur Chronologie und Geschichte des Neuen Reiches* (Wiesbaden, 1964), pp. 71–78, and W. J. Murnane, *Ancient Egyptian Coregencies*, Studies in Ancient Oriental Civilization 40 (Chicago, 1977), pp. 123–169. On the hieratic docket to Amarna Letter 27, see W. Fritz, *Studien zur altägyptischen Kultur* 18 (1991): 207–214.

CHAPTER 3

On the earliest Aten sanctuary at Karnak, whose blocks were reused in the Tenth Pylon, see J.-L. Chappaz, *Bulletin Société d'Égyptologie Genève* 8 (1983): 13–45, and on the blocks from the Ninth Pylon, see especially C. Traunecker, *Journal for the Study of Egyptian Antiquities* 14 (1984): 60–69, and idem, *Bulletin de la Société française d'égyptologie* 107 (1986): 17–44. The *talatat* have been studied by R. W. Smith and D. B. Redford, *The Akhenaten Temple Project*, vol. 1 (Warminster, 1976; and see the critical review by M. Doresse, *Göttinger Miszellen* 46 [1981]: 45–79) and vol. 2 (Toronto, 1988), with further material in the *Cahiers de Karnak*. On the representations of the *sed*-festival, see J. Gohary, *Akhenaten's* Sed-*Festival at Karnak* (London, 1992); a fragmentary *sed*-festival statue of the king from Tod is noted by Ch. Desroches-Noblecourt, *Bulletin de la Société française d'égyptologie* 93 (1982): 18.

The scarab mentioning Amun is published in H. R. Hall, *Catalogue of Egyptian Scarabs, etc., in the British Museum*, vol. 1 (London, 1913), no. 1946 (on "chosen by Amun," see also no. 1945), and see also L. Keimer, *Annales du Service des Antiquités de l'Égypte* 39 (1939): 118; on the unique epithet "son of Amun" on a ring in the Stern collection, see C. Aldred, *Jewels of the Pharaohs* (London, 1971), pl. 70. The stages in the development of the Aten, leading up to his definitive form, have been treated by D. B. Redford, "The Sun-Disc in Akhenaten's Program: Its Worship and Antecedents," *Journal of the American Research Center in Egypt* 13 (1976): 47–61. On other early monuments of the king, see L. Habachi, "Varia from the Time of Akhenaten," *Mitteilungen des Deutschen Archäologischen Instituts, Abteilung Kairo* 20 (1965): 85–92.

H. Schäfer's characterization of Amarna art is to be found in *Amarna in Religion und Kunst* (Leipzig, 1931), pp. 39–40. A. Wiedemann's remarks are from his *Ägyptische Geschichte* (Gotha, 1884), p. 397. For the citation from W. Wolf, see *Die Kunst Ägyptens: Gestalt und Geschichte* (Stuttgart, 1957), p. 453. For the temple wall in the Luxor Museum, see J. Lauffray, *Cahiers de Karnak* VI (1980), foldout plate after p. 74. For the formulation "I am your son who is useful to you and elevates your name," see M. Sandman, *Texts from the Time of Akhenaten*, Bibliotheca Aegyptiaca 8, p. 14, ll. 13–16. On the representations of Akhenaten as a child (of the Aten), see M. Eaton-Krauss, *Zeitschrift für ägyptische Sprache und Altertumskunde* 110 (1983): 127–132.

CHAPTER 4

On the problem of Akhenaten's "teaching," see B. van de Walle in E. Hornung and O. Keel, eds., *Studien zu altägyptischen Lebenslehren*, Orbis Biblicus et Orientalis 28 (Freiburg, 1979), pp. 353–362, and J. Assmann, "Die Loyalistische Lehre Echnatons," *Studien zur altägyptischen Kultur* 8 (1980): 1–32. The royal status of the god is treated by G. Fecht, *Zeitschrift für ägyptische Sprache und Altertumskunde* 85 (1960): 91–118. For the hymn of Panehesy, see M. Sandman, *Texts from the Time of Akhenaten*, Bibliotheca Aegyptiaca 8 (Brussels, 1938), p. 24, ll. 1–7, and see also J. Assmann, *Studien zur altägyptischen Kultur* 8 (1980): 10.

On the role of Shu at Amarna, see B. van de Walle, *Chronique d'Égypte* 55 (1980): 23–36, and now also R. Krauss, *Zeitschrift für ägyptische Sprache und Altertumskunde* 121 (1994): 106–117. For the citation regarding Akhenaten's role as personal god, see J. Assmann, *Studien zur altägyptischen Kultur* 8 (1980): 28, and similar statements in other studies by the same scholar.

For general treatments of Akhenaten's religion, see J. Assmann, "Die 'Häresie' des Echnaton," *Saeculum* 23 (1972): 109–126; idem, *Ägypten— Theologie und Frömmigkeit einer frühen Hochkultur* (Stuttgart, 1984), pp. 232–257; and idem, "Akhanyati's Theology of Light and Time," *Proceedings of the Israel Academy of Sciences and Humanities* VII, no. 4 (Jerusalem, 1992). J. P. Allen has disputed the religious character of Akhenaten's "philosophy," noting that the king himself was considered to be a god; see "The Natural Philosophy of Akhenaten," in W. K. Simpson, ed., *Religion and Philosophy in Ancient Egypt* (New Haven, 1989), pp. 89–101.

The continued veneration of Amenhotpe, son of Hapu, has been treated by D. Wildung, *Imhotep und Amenhotep: Gottwerdung im alten Ägypten,* Münchner ägyptologische Studien 36 (Berlin, 1977).

CHAPTER 5

I have discussed the founding of the new city in my contribution to the Festschrift for Rainer Mackensen: S. Meyer and E. Schulze, eds., *Ein Puzzle, das nie aufgeht: Stadt, Region und Individuum in der Moderne* (Berlin, 1994), pp. 303–308. For a new, improved publication and treatment of the boundary stelae, see W. J. Murnane and C. C. Van Siclen III, *The Boundary Stelae of Akhenaten* (London and New York, 1993). The most recent treatment of the letter of Ipi is by E. F. Wente, *Serapis* 6 (1980): 209–215, and on the foundation, see W. J. Murnane and R. A. Wells, *Studien zur altägyptischen Kultur* 14 (1987): 239–246, 313–333, and also R. Krauss, *Göttinger Miszellen* 103 (1988): 39–44; 109 (1989): 33–36.

On the English excavations, see W. Flinders Petrie, *Tell el Amarna,* Memoirs of the Egypt Exploration Society 38, 40, and 44 (London, 1894); T. E. Peet et al., *The City of Akhenaten,* 3 vols. (London, 1923, 1933, 1951); and the continuing series by B. J. Kemp, *Amarna Reports* (1984–). On the German excavations, see L. Borchardt and H. Ricke,

Die Wohnhäuser in Tell el-Amarna (Berlin, 1980), along with S. Seidl-mayer, *Mitteilungen des Deutschen Archäologischen Instituts Abteilung Kairo* 39 (1983): 183–206 (on the door frames). The fundamental publication of the tombs of the officials remains that of N. de G. Davies, *The Rock Tombs of El Amarna*, Archaeological Survey of Egypt Memoir 13–18 (London, 1903–8).

There are overviews of the city in A. Badawy, *A History of Egyptian Architecture: The Empire (the New Kingdom)* (Berkeley, 1968), pp. 76–126; B. J. Kemp, *Ancient Egypt: Anatomy of a Civilization* (London and New York, 1989), chap. 7; and B. J. Kemp and S. Garfi, *A Survey of the Ancient City of El-Amarna* (London, 1993). On specialized questions, see J. Assmann, "Palast oder Tempel?" *Journal of Near Eastern Studies* 31 (1972): 143–155; J. J. Janssen, "El-Amarna as a Residential City," *Bibliotheca Orientalis* 40 (1983): 273–288; P. T. Crocker, "Status Symbols in the Architecture of El-Amarna," *Journal of Egyptian Archaeology* 71 (1985): 52–65; C. Tietze, "Amarna—Analyse der Wohnhäuser und soziale Struktur der Stadtbewohner," *Zeitschrift für ägyptische Sprache und Altertumskunde* 112 (1985): 48–84; 113 (1986): 55–78; B. J. Kemp, "The Amarna Workmen's Village in Retrospect," *Journal of Egyptian Archaeology* 73 (1987): 21–50; A. H. Bomann, *The Private Chapel in Ancient Egypt* (London and New York, 1991); and A. Endruweit, *Städtischer Wohnbau in Ägypten: Klimagerechte Lehmarchitektur in Amarna* (Berlin, 1994). On the "zoo" in the North Palace, see *Journal of Egyptian Archaeology* 10 (1924): 296; 12 (1926): 5.

CHAPTER 6

For a treatment of the cult in the sanctuaries of the Aten, see A. M. Blackman, in *Receuil d'études égyptologiques dédiées à J. F. Champollion* (Paris, 1922), pp. 505–527; see ibid., pp. 526–527 for the scene from the tomb of Mahu published by Davies, *Rock Tombs*, vol. 4, pl. 18. On the two letters by the "oil-boiler" Ramose, see T. E. Peet, *Annals of Archaeology and Anthropology, University of Liverpool* 17 (1930): 82–97. J. Assmann would translate the second part of the new didactic name differently, as "in his name of the light which comes from the sun"; see *The Search for God in Ancient Egypt* (Ithaca, 2001), p. 210, and similarly in "Akhanyati's Theology of Light and Time," *Proceedings Israel Academy of Sciences and Humanities* VII, no. 4 (1992): 164–165, and *Mono-*

theismus und Kosmotheismus: Ägyptische Formen eines "Denkens des Einen" *und ihre europäische Rezeptionsgeschichte* (Heidelberg, 1993), p. 33 with n. 75. For a detailed treatment of the concept Maat, see J. Assmann, *Ma'at: Gerechtigkeit und Unsterblichkeit im Alten Ägypten* (Munich, 1990).

On the statue in Brooklyn, see R. S. Bianchi, *Göttinger Miszellen* 114 (1990): 35–40, with figure, and also E. Cruz-Uribe, *Göttinger Miszellen* 126 (1992): 29–32, who connects the disk with the moon.

The evidence for Akhenaten from Memphis is treated by B. Löhr, *Studien zur altägyptischen Kultur* 2 (1975): 139–187, and W. Helck, *Studien zur altägyptischen Kultur* 4 (1976): 119–121. On Heliopolis, see L. Habachi, *Beiträge zur ägyptischen Bauforschung und Altertumskunde* 12 (1971): 35–45; H. S. K. Bakry, *Chronique d'Égypte* 47 (1972): 55–67; B. Löhr, *Göttinger Miszellen* 11 (1974): 33–38. For the evidence of traditional religion on the statues of two mayors of Neferusi, see *Urkunden des ägyptischen Altertums*, vol. 4 (Berlin, 1984), pp. 2018–2020.

CHAPTER 7

On the form taken by Egyptian belief in the divine, see E. Hornung, *Die Eine und die Vielen: Altägyptische Gottesvorstellungen*, 3d ed. (Darmstadt, 1993); the first edition has been translated into English by J. Baines under the title *Conceptions of God in Ancient Egypt: The One and the Many* (Ithaca, 1982). The question of monotheism in Akhenaten's religion has been treated many times; see most recently J. Assmann, *Monotheismus und Kosmotheismus: Ägyptische Formen eines "Denkens des Einen" und ihre europäische Rezeptionsgeschichte* (Heidelberg, 1993).

For the dating of the persecution, it is important that we still encounter inscriptions on jars at Tell el-Amarna mentioning a wine maker named Amenemhet; see W. R. Dawson, *Journal of Egyptian Archaeology* 10 (1924): 133. There is as yet no systematic treatment of the persecution, though it certainly left clearly visible traces; only for Karnak has the material been collected by R. Saad, in his unpublished dissertation, *Les martelages de la XVIIIe Dynastie* (Lyon, 1972).

For the first three citations from the Coffin Texts, see, respectively, A. de Buck, *The Egyptian Coffin Texts*, vol. 7, Oriental Institute Publications 87 (Chicago, 1961), p. 158; ibid., vol. 4, Oriental Institute Publications 67 (Chicago, 1951), p. 76; and ibid., vol. 6, Oriental Institute

Publications 81 (Chicago, 1966), p. 319. For Akhenaten's address to Aten, see M. Sandman, *Texts from the Time of Akhenaten*, Bibliotheca Aegyptiaca 8 (Brussels, 1938), p. 46, l. 15. For the final citation from the Coffin Texts, see de Buck, op. cit., vol. 2, Oriental Institute Publications 49 (Chicago, 1951), p. 39.

For various aspects of Amarna religion, and especially the persistence of worship of the traditional deities, see also R. Hari in *Studien zu Sprache und Religion Ägyptens zu Ehren von Wolfhart Westendorf, übbericht von seinen Freunden und Schülern* (Göttingen, 1984), pp. 1039–1055, and K. Bosse-Griffiths, "A Beset Amulet from the Amarna Period," *Journal of Egyptian Archaeology* 63 (1977): 98–106.

CHAPTER 8

Brief surveys of beliefs regarding the afterlife are offered by J. Vandier, *Manuel d'archéologie égyptienne*, vol. 4 (Paris, 1964), pp. 671–674, and E. Hornung, *Zeitschrift für ägyptische Sprache und Altertumskunde* 119 (1992): 125–127. A more detailed evaluation by T. von der Way appeared in *Zeitschrift für ägyptische Sprache und Altertumskunde* 123 (1996): 157–164. Important fundamentals (including the doorjamb of Hatiay) are already to be found in E. Drioton, *Annales du Service des Antiquités de l'Égypte* 43 (1943): 15–43.

On the wish of Suty, see N. de G. Davies, *The Rock Tombs of Amarna*, vol. 4, Memoirs of the Archaeological Survey of Egypt 16, pl. 39 (left post); Huy, etc.: ibid., vol. 3, Memoirs of the Archaeological Survey of Egypt 15, pl. 2, and vol. 4, pl. 3–4; Tutu: ibid., vol. 6, Memoirs of the Archaeological Survey of Egypt 18, pl. 14; Meryre: ibid., vol. 2, Memoirs of the Archaeological Survey of Egypt 14, pl. 36; Ramose: L. Borchardt and H. Ricke, *Die Wohnhäuser in Tell el-Amarna*, Ausgrabungen der Deutschen Orient-Gesellschaft in Tell el Amarna 5 (Berlin, 1980), p. 342, and *Mitteilungen des Deutschen Archäologischen Instituts, Abteilung Kairo* 39 (1983): 196. On the tomb of Aper-El, see A. Zivie, *Découverte à Saqqarah: Le vizir oublié* (Paris, 1990), and *Bulletin de la Société française d'égyptologie* 126 (1993) (several contributions). On the coffin of Taat, see R. Hari, in *Studien zur Sprache und Religion Ägyptens zu Ehren von Wolfhart Westendorf, überreicht von seinen Freunden und Schülern* (Göttingen, 1984), p. 1053. The private *shawabtis* of the Amarna Period are treated by G. T. Martin, *Mitteilungen des Deutschen*

Archäologischen Instituts, Abteilung Kairo 42 (1986): 109–129, though the authenticity of some of them is debatable.

On Akhenaten's tomb and burial equipment, see G. T. Martin, *The Royal Tomb at El-Amarna*, Memoirs of the Archaeological Survey of Egypt 35 and 39 (London, 1974 and 1989), and on the "magical bricks" see E. Thomas, *Journal of the American Research Center in Egypt* 3 (1964): 75–76.

The Judgment of the Dead is treated by Ch. Seeber, *Untersuchungen zur Darstellung des Totengerichts im Alten Ägypten, Münchner ägyptologische Studien* (Munich, 1976).

CHAPTER 9

We still lack a specialized treatment of the late years of Akhenaten, but most of the more important problems are discussed by R. Krauss, *Das Ende der Amarnazeit: Beiträge zur Geschichte und Chronologie des Neuen Reiches*, Hildesheimer ägyptologische Beiträge 7 (Hildesheim, 1978).

On the Nubian campaign, see W. Helck, *Studien zur altägyptischen Kultur* 8 (1980): 117–126. C. Aldred has attempted to explain the foreign tribute as occurring at the beginning of Akhenaten's sole reign, after a rather long coregency with Amenophis III; see *Journal of Egyptian Archaeology* 43 (1957): 114–117.

On Kiya, see R. Hanke, *Amarna-Reliefs aus Hermopolis* (Hildesheim, 1978); Y. Y. Perepelkin, *Kiya and Semenkhkare* (Moscow, 1979) (in Russian); and C. N. Reeves, *Journal of Egyptian Archaeology* 74 (1988): 91–101. On Kiya as the original owner of the canopic jars in Tomb 55, see R. Krauss, *Mitteilungen des Deutschen Archäologischen Instituts, Abteilung Kairo* 42 (1986): 67–80; and on Tomb 55, see also M. Bell, *Journal of the American Research Center in Egypt* 27 (1990): 97–137, which is only one of a large number of studies on this problematic tomb. On Akhenaten's supposed granddaughters, see C. Meyer, *Studien zur altägyptischen Kultur* 11 (1984): 259–263.

The monkey figures from Amarna were published by J. Samson, *Amarna, City of Akhenaten and Nefertiti—Nefertiti as Pharaoh* (Warminster, 1978), pp. 37–40. We have cited Pawah's adoration of Amun from the translation by J. Assmann, *Ägyptische Hymnen und Gebete* (Zurich and Munich, 1975), pp. 349–350 (no. 147).

CHAPTER 10

On the immediate successors of Akhenaten, see R. Krauss, *Das Ende der Amarnazeit: Beiträge zur Geschichte und Chronologie des Neuen Reiches*, Hildesheimer ägyptologische Beiträge 7 (Hildesheim, 1978), and J. Samson, *Amarna, City of Akhenaten and Nefertiti—Nefertiti as Pharaoh* (Warminster, 1978); the stela at University College is treated in ibid., pp. 103–106, but on the uncertainties, see W. J. Murnane, *Journal of Near Eastern Studies* 41 (1982): 143–144, and J. P. Allen, *Journal of the American Research Center in Egypt* 25 (1988): 117–121. A further indication of the coregency is the occurrence together of the double cartouches of Akhenaten and Smenkhkare on a calcite vessel in the treasure of Tutankhamun; see C. E. Loeben, *Bulletin Société d'Égyptologie Genève* 15 (1991): 81–90.

For Tutankhamun, see N. Reeves, *The Complete Tutankhamun: The King, the Tomb, the Royal Treasure* (London, 1990). On the Memphite tomb of Haremhab, which was rediscovered in 1975, see G. T. Martin, *The Memphite Tomb of Horemheb*, vol. 1 (London, 1989). On the recently excavated tomb of Parennefer, see F. Kampp, *Mitteilungen des Deutschen Archäologischen Instituts, Abteilung Kairo* 50 (1994): 175–188, and on the tomb of the tutor Sennedjem at Sohag, see B. G. Ockinga, *A Tomb from the Reign of Tutankhamun at Akhmim*, Australian Centre for Egyptology Reports 10 (Warminster, 1997). Aya has been treated by O. J. Schaden, "The God's Father Ay" (Ph.D. diss. University of Minnesota, 1977); on his rock temple at Akhmim, see K. P. Kuhlmann, *Mitteilungen des Deutschen Archäologischen Instituts, Abteilung Kairo* 35 (1979): 165–188. For Haremhab, see R. Hari, *Horemheb et la reine Moutnedjemet, ou la fin d'une dynastie* (Geneva, 1965), and E. Hornung, *Das Grab des Haremhab im Tal der Könige* (Bern, 1971). For the citation from his "Coronation Inscription" on the group statue in Turin, see *Urkunden des ägyptischen Altertums*, vol. 4 (Berlin, 1984), pp. 2119–2120.

CHAPTER 11

On the influence of Amarna religion on Israel, see V. A. Tobin, "Amarna and Biblical Religion," in S. Israelit-Groll, ed., *Pharaonic Egypt, the Bible and Christianity* (Jerusalem, 1985), pp. 231–277, who treats the commonalities and differences, and K. Koch, *Geschichte der ägyptischen Religion von den Pyramiden bis zu den Mysterien der Isis* (Stuttgart, 1993), pp. 348–350, who rejects an influence on Moses, because the sun played no special role for the latter. There are also the collaborative volumes O. Keel, ed., *Monotheismus im Alten Israel und seiner Umwelt,* Biblische Beiträge NS 14 (Freiburg, 1980), and K. Rahner, ed., *Der eine Gott und der dreieine Gott: Das Gottesverständnis bei Christen, Juden und Muslimen* (Freiburg, 1983). On the comparison between the "Great Hymn to the Aten" and Psalm 104, see P. Auffret, *Hymnes d'Égypte et d'Israel: Études de structures littéraires,* Orbis Biblicus et Orientalis 34 (Freiburg and Göttingen, 1981), and J. Assmann, *Proceedings Israel Academy of Sciences and Humanities* VII, no. 4 (1992), pp. 166–168.

The citation from Assmann is from *Saeculum* 23 (1972): 125, and that from the hymn of Tjanefer from idem, *Ägyptische Hymnen und Gebete* (Zurich and Munich, 1975), no. 108. On Tutankhamun's "Enigmatic Book of the Netherworld," see E. Hornung, *Journal of the Society for the Study of Egyptian Antiquities* 13 (1983): 29–34, and on the "Book of the Heavenly Cow," idem, *Der ägyptische Mythos von der Himmelskuh: Eine Ätiologie des Unvollkommenen,* 2d ed. (Freiburg and Göttingen, 1991). For Huy's lament, see *Urkunden des ägyptischen Altertums,* vol. 4 (Berlin, 1984), p. 2076. On the representation of the new god Shed already at Amarna, see H. Brunner, *Göttinger Miszellen* 78 (1984): 49–50.

Index